a spectator's guide

world views

EDITED BY SIMON SMART

blue bottle
BOOKS

PO Box A 287, Sydney South, Australia 1235
Ph: (02) 8268 3333
Fax: (02) 8268 3357
Email: sales@youthworks.net

A spectator's guide to worldviews—ten ways of understanding life
Published June 2007
National Library of Australia ISBN 978 1 921137 77 8
Copyright 2007© Blue Bottle Books

Designed and typeset by Nicole Gillan

Steve Turner Poem *Creed* © Steve Turner 1980. Reprinted by permission of the author and the Lisa Eveleigh Literary Agency.

Song Lyrics *I'm so Postmodern* © Justin Heazlewood (aka The Bedroom Philosopher) used by kind permission.

contents

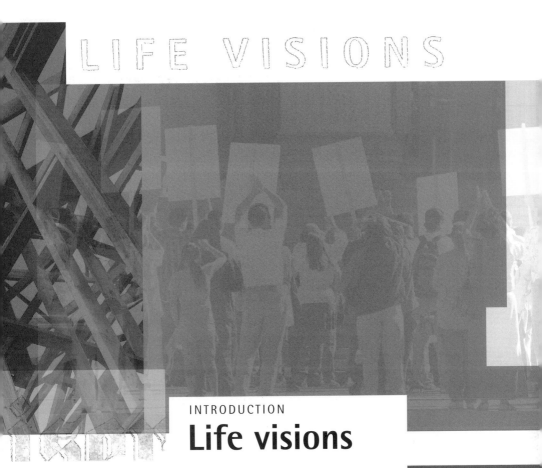

INTRODUCTION
Life visions

Simon Smart

WHAT IS A WORLDVIEW?

> Our worldview acts as the lens through which we view the world.

Pick up any newspaper in any city or town and you will witness a collision of different worlds. There isn't a day that goes by without a report of controversy, debate, violence, scandal and conflict between individuals and among nations. These range from minor disputes to catastrophic events. To be human involves bumping up against other humans who see the world very differently to us. No matter how hard we try to avoid it, nothing can protect us from that reality. When confronted with this in both subtle and direct ways, many of us can feel threatened, afraid, anxious or perhaps angry.

This book examines a series of highly influential systems of thought, each of which represents [the whole or part of] a distinct way of looking at the world. Each is the articulation of a worldview. The term 'worldview' comes from the German word *Weltanschauung*. It is a word social commentators like to toss around. We may be unaware of it, but each of us has a worldview. It is an important concept to grapple with in order to understand more about ourselves, our world and other people.

A worldview may be understood as a framework or set of fundamental beliefs through which we view the world and our place in it.[1] This framework could be thought of as being like the frame of a house[2] —that is not seen, but is crucial to the way our reality is constructed and held together. It supports our beliefs, our actions, and our plans and hopes for the future. It gives shape to our lives and creates the space in which we live and speak, act and dream. This frame is our frame. It might be the same as some, but is very different from others.

Our worldview acts as the lens through which we view the world. We might not look *at* the lens, but we do look *through* it, and it will largely determine what we see in front of us. That lens can be very different for different people, and produce vastly divergent ways of understanding reality.

In the diagram below the same scene is viewed by three different people. What person A sees through the lens (their worldview) is totally different to person C, and different (although closer) to person B.

This is a little like what is meant when we consider the nature of different and conflicting worldviews. They present to us a vision of the world and reality that is distinct and in some cases very different to others.

Writers on the topic tend to pin down a number of themes that help us to describe a particular worldview.[3] As we begin to focus on these you might like to think about your own answers to these questions.

reality

What is the nature of the universe and the world around us?

Is there a God or gods; is there a spiritual realm or is the universe merely made up of physical matter?

Was the world created with order and a plan, or chaotic and the result of blind chance?

human nature

What is a human being—a highly developed animal, a complex machine, a unique creation of God made in his image, a spark from an eternal flame, or a combination of ever changing physical and mental activities?

death

What happens to people when they die? Do they return in a different form; does their soul become one with the universe; do they simply cease to exist or do they face eternal life with or without God? Is there another possibility?

knowing

How and what can we know? How can we know anything at all? Is it because consciousness has evolved over millions of years, or because God who is relational allows us to have knowledge and consciousness as his special created beings?

value

How do we know what is right and wrong? Is it because we are subjects of God who is good; is 'right and wrong' merely human choice; is it embedded in a natural law that is true for all time and all places; or is right and wrong merely the result of actions connected to the process of survival of the fittest?

purpose

What is the meaning of human history? Is it to participate in the purposes of God; to live full, busy and happy lives; to be in community with others; to create paradise on earth; to leave the world a better place?

The answers that we give to these questions provide an indication of the worldview that we hold.

James Sire, who has spent decades thinking about how to describe worldviews, drawing on the work of Walsh and Middleton, suggests that a person's worldview may be discovered in the answer they give to four key questions[4]:

i. **Who am I?** What is the nature and task of human beings?

ii. **Where am I?** What is the nature of the world and universe that I live in? Do I see the world and universe as personal, ordered and controlled; or chaotic, cruel and random?

iii. **What's wrong?** Why is it that my world appears to be *not the way it's supposed to be*? How do I make sense of evil?

iv. **What is the solution?** Where do I find hope for something better?

A VISION FOR LIFE

Beginning to reflect on these frameworks or fundamental beliefs about the world, we might ask 'What type of worldview would lead someone to strap an explosive device to themselves, and detonate it in a crowded market?'. Admittedly this is an extreme example but it highlights the way one worldview can be radically different from others, and immensely powerful as a motivator of action. In fact worldviews are most easily identified in our actions. The way we live exposes much about our beliefs.

What might be the worldview of the CEO whose priority at work lies with the forces of the market and the interests of shareholders? He will justify retrenching large numbers of workers with dependent families on the grounds of profit and efficiency and he rests easy with his decisions.

When a scientist works in her laboratory carrying out tests and experiments she does so with a belief that the universe is orderly and consistently follows set patterns of cause and effect. In fact she could not carry out the experiments without such a belief. Her understanding of just where that orderliness comes from may well be very different to the person sitting at the desk next to her. Behind her actions, and her planning and testing lies a belief that the world is a certain way and not other ways.

A father praying at the bedside of his sick daughter; a woman who decides to leave her marriage soon after it becomes difficult with little regret over her decision; a couple who leave a comfortable existence in the West to work as doctors in the slums of Bangladesh; a man who spends his life's energy acquiring larger houses, cars and boats; a lawyer who defends known criminals; and a family who together attend an anti-war demonstration all behave in ways that reflect some aspect of their worldview. Somewhere as the backdrop to the way we live, lies our understanding of reality—our worldview.

James Olthuis says a person's worldview describes not just the way things are, but the way they ought to be. In this way, worldview acts as both a vision *of* life and a vision *for* life.[5] It serves as a way of processing the world as we encounter it and gives us a picture of truth, answering the biggest questions in life and pointing to some sort of salvation.[6]

It might be helpful to think of worldview as the *story that we live by*,[7] with the story providing a kind of ultimate interpretation of reality.[8] So for Christians, the grand story of the Bible, of **Creation**, **the fall** of humanity, **redemption** through Jesus Christ and the world headed towards **new creation,** provides the framework within which people can live their life with meaning and purpose.

Of course not everyone accepts that particular story, but nonetheless we all have a degree of faith or commitment to one story or another. The atheistic scientist relies on her faith in the story of science to explain all of life and the nature of the universe. The Buddhist monk holds to a story that explains existence and the trajectory each person is on. Some people might hold to a very limited story —just the story of their own life, without thinking much about the larger questions of existence, but they are choosing to live out a story. Even for the Postmodernist who consciously rejects all large narratives (more on that later in this book), that too is a story that they live by—albeit a more difficult story to live in any consistent fashion.

HISTORY

When thinking about the way 'big ideas' shape a society it is important to understand that these ideas change and develop over time. Worldview is thus heavily influenced by our place and time in history. For instance if you lived in the Western world prior to 1700 it is highly likely that you would have believed in the reality of the supernatural, absolute truth, and the dependence of humanity, nature and all of society on God's overriding control. You might not have been a Christian but the above beliefs would have been self-evident to you and those around you.[9] You would almost certainly have been less conscious of yourself as an individual and had a greater sense of identity in the community you were a part of. This was an age of 'pre-modern theism'.

From around the 1700s remarkable achievements in science and exploration led human beings to have confidence they could take control of their destiny. The age of 'modernism' flourished in the 'Enlightenment' and peaked in the twentieth century. During this time the power of rationalism and human autonomy became the dominant (although not exclusive) mode of thinking. This was expressed in rejection of the supernatural, belief in a mechanistic closed universe and unbounded enthusiasm for the self-styled progress of humankind.

Disillusionment with modernism has, since about the 1960s brought in an age referred to as postmodernism, now extremely influential in contemporary life. More openness to spiritual realms and extreme suspicion of any claim to absolute truth are just two examples of the way postmodernism has influenced Western society.

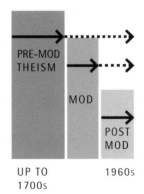

PRE-MOD THEISM

MOD

POST MOD

UP TO 1700s

1960s

This diagram first appeared in the work of Julie Mitchell in *Teaching about Worldviews and Values*, (The Council for Christian Education in Schools, Melbourne Australia, 2004), page 10.

The above patterns are generalisations, but they outline a broad shape of the way Western thought has evolved and changed over time. These patterns are significant for at least two related reasons:

i.   The changes that have occurred in worldviews over centuries indicate just how much we are influenced by the culture in which we live. This knowledge should help us to see why it is wise to be conscious of and critical towards the major influences that shape our own worldview and understanding of reality —and of course that includes the Christian worldview. We need to be discerning and self-reflective when it comes to the big questions of life.

ii.   The Christian worldview, while finding different expressions and emphases over the centuries has remained unchanged at its core. What a Christian living in West Africa today shares with a follower of Jesus in Manhattan or Gunnedah or Saskatoon, they each share with a Christian who lived in fourth century Athens. The key foundational beliefs of the Christian worldview remain the same today. That at least should cause us to give it the careful consideration that its place in history deserves. We might reject it entirely, but we need to know what it is that we are rejecting, and what we have taken on instead as the true nature of the world and our existence.

Each of us holds a worldview that has come to us through many and varied influences. Our individual personalities contribute to the way we filter the information that comes to us from the earliest age. We are no doubt deeply impacted by external realities such as our socioeconomic situation, the traditions we have been brought up in, our experience of relationships with family and friends, our emotions, temperament, sexuality, health and education. Further, our experience of institutions such as marriage, family and government are significant.[10] As such, James Sire explains that our definition of worldview takes in 'the totality of human psychological existence – the way we think and view reality, our appraisal of life, and the way we act revealing our worldview,' and is what he describes as a 'life system'.[11]

WHY THINK ABOUT WORLDVIEWS?

The influence of various worldviews is all around us. It is in the air we breathe. Every time we listen to a song, see a film, view a piece of art, read a newspaper feature-article, hear or see an advertisement, listen to the radio, read a novel, listen to a speech, watch a TV program, read a poem, view a sit-com, or engage in a conversation with friends we are being exposed to a worldview of some kind or other. Key thinkers in society, professors, educationalists, doctors, politicians and community leaders all have a worldview that reveals itself in their actions and words. The school curriculum that each of us is exposed to comes out of a carefully thought-out philosophy that is different today to the one that students were exposed to in the 1980s, which was different again to the previous generation. None of the changes are accidental – each emerges out of the worldview of those in the educational driving seat at the time.

We would do well to seek to understand the influence various worldviews have on us, and the foundation on which they are built. It is in our interest to think carefully about our own worldview and to test its validity.

David Naugle recommends three tests to understand whether a worldview is sustainable:

1. coherence test

Do the propositions of the worldview agree with each other or are they contradictory?[12] For instance would it make sense to say that we believe only in a closed universe (meaning there is no room for the supernatural or transcendent) and yet stand at the grave of a friend and talk of them now being a part of nature or somehow looking down on the world?

Does your system of belief fit together in a consistent manner?

2. reality test

Does the worldview in question fit with reality and is it capable of giving satisfactory explanations for the totality of things? Are large chunks of the human experience left out?[13]

For example, is it satisfactory to talk of the human personality being a complex machine primarily determined by genetic makeup that controls virtually everything about a person? Does such an understanding adequately explain the feeling of being in love, or bitterly angry at injustice, or heartbroken by suffering and loss?

3. pragmatic test

Does the worldview work? Can you live the worldview in question? Can it be applied to human experience and does it have something meaningful to say about key concerns and issues of life?[14]

Does this worldview have something to say in answer to the questions that I have about purpose and hope, and how I gain identity and meaning?

A spectator's guide to worldviews asks you to consider systems of thought that have played major roles in shaping the society in which we operate in the West. Not every chapter here deals with a fully-orbed worldview. Yet each has played and continues to play an influential role in the way people think in Western society. Each represents a way of thinking and a theory about life that emanates from worldviews. For example, the chapters on humanism, modernism, and to an extent, liberalism and utilitarianism, emerge from a worldview we might describe as *naturalism*—or the belief that the physical universe is all there is—there is no God and it is up to us as human beings to make the best of life without guidance from outside. People in contemporary Western culture appear able to hold on to a mix of different philosophies and influences that may be inconsistent, contradictory or at least not a neatly packaged system of belief.

The writers of each chapter hold firmly to a Christian worldview although they will aim to give a balanced, fair and objective presentation of each 'ism'. There will be an attempt to highlight where each topic finds common ground or agreement with Christian thought and where they are distinct or in some cases directly opposed. We hope that in carefully examining each topic so as to understand something of its basis and the implications of accepting it as true, readers will be in a better position to make their own judgments. On each occasion you will be able to compare and recognise distinctions with Christianity and to judge which ones look more likely to pass the test of coherence, reality and liveability.

Our increasingly complex society is one in which we operate in close proximity with people at work, in our neighbourhood, on the bus, in classrooms and possibly in the same house who regard our own worldview as nonsense.[15] All the more important is the need to understand and articulate our own worldviews—what we believe about God, ourselves, other people and the world around us.

David Naugle says that worldviews 'set the interior spaces of the human heart, determine thoughts and actions, set the course of local culture and entire civilisations for good or ill'.[16]

If we are to become thoughtful, discerning members of a global community we will need to be able to evaluate and critique our own society as well as others. To do this well we will benefit from understanding something of the worldviews of others by being informed and conscious of what lies behind the messages we receive.

We need to understand our own worldview if we are to know where we stand and not be buffeted by every message we are hit with.

It is the conviction of this writer and all those contributing to the book, that there is no more comprehensive, hopeful and compelling story than the Christian story and the answers it gives to each of the questions of coherence, reality and liveability, and dare we say it—truth! It is our hope that as you read through these important shaping influences of Western thought you will make considered comparisons and thoughtful evaluation of a Christian worldview as it relates to others, and importantly your own.

It is a journey worth taking, and we wish you well as you embark upon it.

Given that a major goal of this book is to compare Christianity with some of the alternative worldviews on offer today, we need to begin in Chapter One with a brief account of the biblical way of thinking about life, the world and each other. Of course, the Christian worldview begins with God.

confusion reigns

Matt thought his head would explode. How much longer did he have to listen to this stuff? A group assignment for Psychology 101 on 'access to the pre-conscious mind, in Freud's "the interpretation of Dreams (1899)" didn't exactly turn him on, and that was without being thrown into this group of misfits. Just his luck in a class of 300 to be drawn at random to be in a group that included not a single person he could relate to. His mind began to drift towards more palatable topics—meeting Suzie on Thursday night, rugby practice later tonight, and the game on Saturday.

'*Hello* dreamer boy', snapped Lisa. 'Feel free to join in here.' Matt felt his face flush as he stammered some excuse before retreating into silence. Lisa Ward was a second year Social Work student perpetually dressed in black and purple. It was impossible to imagine her wearing anything else. Adorned with piercings sufficient to give her otherwise unremarkable face a look that simultaneously drew intrigue and intimidation—her entire demeanour was like her interpretation of a uniform for the dispossessed.

But Matt knew that Lisa came from the same leafy area of the city as he did. She had gone to his sister's school and so could hardly claim the moral high ground reserved for the truly trampled. Yet none of this had prevented her from berating Matt at their first meeting as being the product of a bourgeois factory of capitalist oppressors; an old-school-tie boy who would perpetuate moronic middle class morality that would leave him brain-dead but sleeping at the top of the heap nonetheless. 'What was she talking about?' thought Matt, desperately and fruitlessly searching for a comeback.

And here he was late on Tuesday afternoon in the student union cafeteria slumped over a warm beer and cold pizza in a booth with six others trying to cobble together an assignment on a topic he knew nothing about and cared even less for. Matt knew that he wasn't alone in his disinterest—at least Brad was here sharing the apathy. It was more than the present dilemma that was bothering Matt though. The whole first semester was messing with his head with an irresistible force.

Life since school was proving to be very different to what he'd anticipated. The summer parties were rapidly fading into a nostalgic past. The whole university thing was beginning to unnerve him. He'd never met so many people with such a different take on life. He'd always been popular, laid-back and on for a laugh. He had breezed through school without busting a gut, immersed in a life that was comfortable and familiar like an old pair of boots. Life was straightforward and fun.

Here he was in the first semester of an Arts/Law degree and his world was beginning to unravel. He didn't even really know why he was doing the degree. 'Couldn't think of what else to do really?' he'd responded lamely to the Master of his residential college. That feeling of uncertainty was not lessened by moments such as the one he was having now.

Beside him was Francesca, a tiny Italian majoring in English literature and scarily smart. She was nicer than Lisa but didn't seem to regard Matt with any degree of seriousness. That too he wasn't used to.

'Freud's take on the unconscious was true for him, and many others, so even though some of his work has been discredited, it was true for its day', she announced. Matt who was yet to learn to control an unfortunate habit of thinking out loud, spoke over the top of Nigel when he blurted, 'Surely it's either true or it isn't?'

The silence and withering looks of disbelief that greeted this gem of insight Matt thought befitting someone attacking Mother Teresa.

Brad, who appeared to have come from at least the same universe as Matt, and who had possibly contributed even less to the group's work so far, suddenly spoke up. 'Well all that stuff about sexual repression and wanting to possess your parents in the Freud doco in class is the biggest load of crap I've ever heard—he hasn't seen *my* mother!'

'Brad that's just your aesthetic', countered Nigel in a voice at once serene, authoritative and dismissive. 'I'm more interested in the way Freud used language to challenge power structures and to establish some of his own.' Brad who had no idea what Nigel was talking about, shook his head and smirked at the others for support. He didn't receive any.

Jean now spoke for the first time today. Of Malaysian descent, Jean had been born here and had a local accent that appeared incongruous with her exotic looks. 'I say Freud was right about all that repressed sexual energy. Christians are like that—that's why they are all so intense and uptight.'

Just what this had to do with anything Matt couldn't fathom, but it drew a laugh from the group. Strangely he found himself wanting to defend his one or two Christian friends who weren't anything like what Jean described.

He didn't consider himself particularly religious but had a nodding acquaintance with God that became more intimate whenever he was in any sort of trouble. He knew Jean was into just about every religion on the block. He'd remembered that from their first conversation. She'd said how much she enjoyed O-week and all the different religious groups on campus being represented. According to Jean all religions have something of beauty and truth and ultimately lead to the one place.

Somehow her generous approach didn't seem to extend to Christianity however.

Finally Jeff spoke up and rescued the afternoon from being a total waste of time. A student of business and accounting, Matt never found out why Jeff was doing Psychology, but on this occasion he was glad he did. Jeff took control, assigned readings and tasks to each person and adjourned the meeting to resume in a week's time.

Matt couldn't wait to get out of there and exiting the building he was surprised to find Jeff at his elbow. 'Hey listen, don't freak out about all this stuff. It's just a means to an end you know. You've got to get it done and get out of here. You've just got to learn to play the game. At the end of the day we're here for a piece of paper—so don't forget that.'

That sounded encouraging but didn't seem to help. Matt had a growing sense of unease that he couldn't explain and didn't understand himself. In some sense all of the things he had taken for granted up until now were being challenged. Some of what he was hearing and learning he really liked the sound of —but other things seemed ridiculous. The problem was he was beginning to doubt himself.

Talking to Suzie hadn't helped. She was working in the city and appeared immune to most of the things Matt found himself daily having to wrestle with. Besides, even Suzie was starting to freak Matt out with her sudden interest in crystals, self-actualisation and inner spirituality. She was reading all this New Age stuff that people at her work were into. So far, Matt's issues weren't getting much empathy from her.

Matt sensed their worlds were slowly being wrenched apart with glacial force. This suspicion was given more weight when Suzie joined a committee of work colleagues planning a Christmas festival that would reconstitute the festive season for modern spiritual practices. 'Christmas means different things to different people', Suzie explained. 'We just want to explore that and take Christmas to a new level.' Matt didn't allow himself to wonder what sort of 'level' a committee of Suzie's might come up with that could supersede the concept of God himself becoming a human being!

It is fair to say that Matt was experiencing an existential wobble—a worldview crisis, as the things he had taken for granted about the world or thought little of, were being challenged in ways he hadn't anticipated. He longed for familiarity and simpler days when he and his mates saw things in pretty much the same way. The promise and optimism of the road ahead still looked inviting—but potholes, twists and turns loomed large in the frame.**SS**

CHAPTER 1

God's signposts: THE CHRISTIAN WORLDVIEW

John Dickson

GOD
the basis of the Christian Worldview

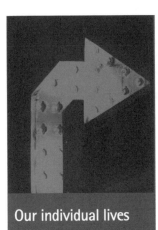

Our individual lives will only find their true purpose when we connect with our source, God.

Belief in God is a common feature of the human experience. Like the fascination with art and music, or our quest for intimacy and social organisation, reverence for a Creator is one of the few shared traits of the whole human family. Even today, four out of five Australians acknowledge the existence of God; only about 1 one in 20 people describe themselves as atheists.[1]

The proposition that *God exists* is not provable in a mathematical sense, nor can it be tested by science— science, by definition, can only assess objects and phenomena that belong to the physical universe.

And God, by definition, is *not* part of the universe. He stands behind it as its Originator and above it as its Preserver. A moment's thought reveals that quite a lot of 'truths' are beyond the reach of empirical testing. Most judgments in a court of law are made without reference to scientific proofs (unless DNA or ballistics happen to be involved). Almost all historical knowledge is the same: what we know about the beliefs of the Egyptian Pharaohs, the life of Plato or the economics of ancient Rome comes from data that cannot be verified by any scientific test. Does this then mean we don't really 'know' this stuff? Of course not. Many truths lie outside the realm of science.

While some religious believers attempt to *prove* that God exists, many Christian philosophers are content simply to affirm that God's existence *explains* the universe we live in better than God's non-existence. How so? A universe that 'banged' into existence with sophisticated and elegant laws of physics already in place (as cosmologists remind us was the case), is more likely to be the result of a great 'Mind' than a big accident. Add to this the fact that this universe (through these physical laws) has eventually produced beings like us, with minds that can grasp these laws, and the 'accident' theory seems even less satisfying. In short, we have just the sort of universe you'd expect if there is a Creator behind it and the kind of universe you could never expect if there isn't. This does not prove God's existence but it goes some way toward explaining why, without proof, most people throughout history have believed in some kind of God.

The existence of a Creator is the premise of the Christian worldview. It is the ultimate assumption and it informs everything else. For Christians, the physical cosmos and human beings within it are the deliberate creation of one Lord. Life is no accident; it was intended. Our individual lives, therefore, will only find their true purpose when we connect with our Source, God.

GOD AND THE HISTORY OF JESUS:
the nature of Christian revelation

The simple fact of worldwide reverence for a Maker raises some obvious questions. How do we know what this Grand Mind is like? Whose god should we listen to? Perhaps there is a spiritual kingdom beyond the material one, but which version of it should we seek?

Deists accept the existence of a great Mind behind the universe, but they leave it there, assuming nothing more can be said (Albert Einstein was a deist). Hinduism declares that the path to Brahman (ultimate reality), as revealed in the Bhagavad-Gita, is to devote oneself to one of Brahman's emanations—Siva, Vishnu, and so on. Islam counters that the Quran revealed to the Prophet Muhammad is God's Word, the straight path back to the divine. At this point many throw up their hands and say, 'God is a mystery. Stories of his appearance on the human stage amount to little more than claim and counter-claim'!

The Christian worldview offers a solution to the quest for clarity about the Maker.

The unique and enduring claim of Christianity in all its forms is that the God of universal conviction has broken into history for all to see. The 'kingdom of God' has touched the world of humanity in a tangible way. While churches have disagreed about many things through the centuries, the acknowledged core of Christianity is Jesus Christ, his teaching, healings, death and rising to life. And all of these—including the healings and resurrection—remain the subject of serious examination by scholars today. Because Christianity's claims are tangible, having to do with historical events, not simply timeless spiritual truths, they are probed and evaluated in a manner without parallel in the study of the world religions. And, when scrutinised, Christianity fares much better than most of us realise.[2]

The point of all this is to emphasise that, for Christians, God has become involved in human history. He has revealed himself to us not in a private insight of a lone guru, nor a divine dictation to a solo prophet. The Christian revelation is fundamentally historical—it is about events that occurred in time and space recorded by a multiplicity of witnesses. In the life of Jesus Christ, God has broken onto the world stage for all to see and he has left a trail of historical evidence which, while not amounting to clear 'proof', is nonetheless compelling. In Christ alone, says the Christian worldview, can it be reasonably stated that the God of our universal hunch has left us a tangible sign of his interest in us as well as a signpost back to him.

So, what do we read when we walk up close to the signpost? What does the life of Jesus tell us about God, ourselves and the world?

JESUS AS HEALER:
why Christians are people of hope

As soon as we open the Gospels, the first century accounts of his life, we are confronted with the claim that Jesus restored the sight of the blind, healed the sick and exercised mastery over nature itself. He performed what one non-Christian source from the first century describes as 'inexplicable deeds'.[3] While the *non*-Christian references to Jesus corroborate his fame as a wonder-worker, can such claims be believed today?

How we answer this question depends not only on historical evidence, which in the case of Jesus' miracles is good, but also on our underlying beliefs about God.

If we assume that the observable laws of nature are the only things governing the universe—that there is no Lawgiver behind these laws, no God—then claims of miracles, no matter how widespread the historical evidence, logically will be dismissed as nonsense. If, on the other hand, we hold that the laws of nature are not the only things governing the universe—and believe instead that there is a Lawgiver, or God, behind the laws of nature—then, given the strength of the historical evidence in this case, openness to Jesus' miracles is perfectly rational.[4]

More important for the Christian worldview than the above philosophical observation is an understanding of the *meaning* of Christ's reported deeds. According to Jesus, his healings were a tangible sign that 'the kingdom of God has come' (Matthew 12:28). This is an important idea; so let's explore it a little.

The 'Kingdom of God' was first promised in the Old Testament, or Jewish Scriptures. There it is pledged that God will one day overthrow evil and heal our frailty, and so prove himself King over his creation. If you have ever found yourself asking, 'Why doesn't God do something about the evil and pain of our world?', you have, in a sense, hoped for what Jesus called the Kingdom.

Strikingly, Jesus insisted that his healings, exorcisms and mastery over nature were not simply an indication of his kingly status in God's Kingdom. Jesus' miracles were a *preview* of the Kingdom itself —they were the trailer for the coming blockbuster. His deeds were a pledge within history that what we all yearn for—the triumph of justice and the renewal of human life—God will one day accomplish in his kingdom. The kingdom is not 'heaven' exactly, as people often understand it, but what the Bible calls a 'new creation' (Revelation 21), a place where all of the disorder and pain and sorrow is replaced with order and wholeness and joy.

The Christian worldview, then, not only looks backwards to the events of Jesus in the past; it looks forward to what those events promise. Christians are people of immense hope—or, at least, they are meant to be. They have glimpsed the future in the wonderful deeds of Christ and soldier on through life confident that, come what may, God will one day make everything new, just as Jesus did in his ministry.

This doesn't mean the Christian worldview is all about pie-in-the-sky when you die. Those who have glimpsed the future in the healing deeds of Jesus also commit themselves to serving the world, just as he did, in whatever way they can this side of God's kingdom. They relieve suffering at every opportunity and resist evil wherever they see it. The creation of Christian hospitals and hospices in fourth century Rome and the (largely Christian) movement to abolish slavery in eighteenth century England are just two historical examples of this logic. We don't yet possess all the resources of the 'kingdom come', says the Christian, but we do know the aims of the kingdom—to renew human life and put an end to evil—and these are to shape what we strive for from day to day. The Christian worldview is about both *hope* for the future and *action* here and now.

JESUS AS TEACHER AND JUDGE:
the Christian view of humanity

Jesus the Healer was also famous as a teacher. Many of his sayings have become proverbial in Western culture: 'Turn the other cheek' (Matthew 5: 39), 'Do to others what you would have them do to you', (Matthew 7:12), 'You are the salt of the earth' (Matthew 5:13), 'It is more blessed to give than to receive' (Acts 20:35) and countless other examples.

But what is the central obligation of men and women, according to Jesus? When asked this question he replied: ' "Love the Lord your God with all your heart and with all your soul and with all your mind". This is the first and greatest commandment. And the second is like it: "Love your neighbour as yourself ",' (Matthew 22:37–39).

According to Jesus Christ, the Golden Rule of God's Kingdom is a simple, two-fold directive: love your Maker and love your neighbour. This recalls the fundamental notion of being made in God's image (Genesis 1:26–27). This doesn't mean we actually look like God; it simply means that human beings reflect God's glory and purposes in the world. This means each of us has an obligation to honour both God (in whose image we are created) and other people (who share that image). The logic is seamless. If God exists, what could be more basic to authentic human life than wholehearted devotion to our Creator and selfless care for our fellow creatures!

Jesus' teaching above leaves no room either for the *religious hypocrite,* who is zealous for God but uncaring toward others, or the *ethical agnostic* who aims to be a 'good person' but ignores the Creator himself. Both fail the teaching of Christ. Both fail to recognise we are made in the image of God.

Our culture rightly condemns those who 'love God' but lack basic human compassion. In doing so, however, we should recognise that the reverse is equally contemptible, from Christ's perspective. Loving our neighbour while shunning the Creator is a grave distortion of the shape of human life. It is to break what Jesus called 'the first and greatest commandment'. Such a person may be 'good' on his or her definition, but not on Christ's.

It is because of this logic that the Christian worldview has a healthy scepticism about the 'goodness' of humanity. While some like to think of humans as *basically good* (and others get rid of the notion of 'good' altogether), Christians follow the teaching of Jesus in affirming that all of us —including Christians—are 'sinners'.

The word 'sin' has bad press. In popular usage it often means nothing more than those petty vices some people get up to—swearing, getting drunk, having multiple sexual partners and so on. The biblical word 'sin' (Greek: *hamartia*) is much deeper. It really means 'to miss' or 'go astray'. In light of Jesus' twofold Golden Rule, to sin is to *fail* to revere God as we should and to care for others as they deserve. When Christians speak of themselves and others as 'sinners', they are not saying we swear too much or don't go to church enough or that we aren't likable people. They mean what Jesus meant: that men and women have a universal obligation to love their Maker with all their heart and to love their neighbours as themselves. Instead of doing that, we 'go astray' from it.

This is why there was such urgency in Jesus' mission and (as you may have noticed) in the mission of Christians today. Christ said God is going to judge us for our sin. This is an unpopular idea (even more unpopular than the word 'sin'); the preferred God for many today is the vague, distant Creator who kick-started the universe but who now, if he thinks of us at all, warmly approves of most of what we do. But, according to Jesus, when God establishes his Kingdom and puts everything right in the world, he will condemn all that is opposed to his just purposes. This will include ethical agnosticism no less than religious hypocrisy. The command to love God and neighbour, then, is not simply the shape of an authentic life; it is the criterion of divine judgment.

If sin and judgment are the bad news of the Christian worldview, the good news is what God has done to invite us into his kingdom regardless of our unworthiness.

JESUS' DEATH AND RESURRECTION:
Christianity's offer to the world

Christ's extraordinary life ended abruptly and in apparent failure with his public execution. Crucifixion was the Roman Empire's *summum supplicium*, 'ultimate punishment', usually reserved for political dissidents. No one could talk of a coming 'kingdom' and of his central place in it without provoking the wrath of Rome.[5]

Political explanations tell only part of the story. Far from being a failure, Christ's death was the ultimate expression of God's justice and compassion. It was the means by which God the Judge could show mercy to the guilty.

On the eve of his execution, as he shared one Last Supper with his followers, Jesus spoke of his imminent death as a sacrifice which would guarantee God's forgiveness and open up to us God's Kingdom:

> While they were eating, Jesus took bread, gave thanks and broke it, and gave it to his disciples, saying, "Take and eat; this is my body." Then he took the cup, gave thanks and offered it to them, saying, "Drink from it, all of you. This is my blood of the covenant, which is poured out for many for the forgiveness of sins. I tell you, I will not drink of this fruit of the vine from now on until that day when I drink it anew with you in my Father's kingdom".

MATTHEW 26:26-29

Within hours, Jesus' blood would indeed be poured out, not as a simple act of martyrdom but as a willing substitute for those facing judgment. By Christ's sacrificial death, we who have failed God's twofold obligation—to love the Creator and care for our fellow creatures—may be freely forgiven: more than that, may share with Christ in his 'Father's kingdom'.

It is because of this that Christians never despair of themselves and humanity. They are keenly aware that God's capacity for mercy and forgiveness far exceeds our capacity for doing good, for fulfilling the universal twofold obligation. This provides believers with a robust self-esteem. They know that despite their failures they are loved by God, pardoned by him and assured of a place after death in his wonderful kingdom. None of this is because of the Christian's moral deeds; it is all because the Healer and Teacher is also the Saviour who died.

He is also the Lord who rose again. Contrary to all expectations of the day, Jesus' followers insisted that their crucified Saviour had been raised from the dead. Their claim, for which many of them gave their lives, launched a movement that would utterly transform the world.

Mainstream scholars agree on three things: (a) the claims about Jesus' resurrection were immediate, not part of a developing legend; (b) the tomb of Jesus was empty shortly after his burial; (c) significant numbers of witnesses claimed to have seen him risen from the dead.[6] As with miracles generally, how we interpret this data depends not so much on historical evidence, which in the case of these three points is very strong, but on those underlying convictions about God.

The first Christians' convictions about God were unshakeable. They had no hesitation in declaring that their Teacher, Healer and Saviour had been raised to life as Lord and God. The point is powerfully stated in one of the resurrection scenes of John's Gospel:

> A week later his disciples were in the house again, and Thomas was with them. Though the doors were locked, Jesus came and stood among them and said, "Peace be with you!" Then he said to Thomas, "Put your finger here; see my hands. Reach out your hand and put it into my

side. Stop doubting and believe." Thomas said to him, "My Lord and my God!" Then Jesus told him, 'because you have seen me, you have believed; blessed are those who have not seen and yet have believed".'

JOHN 20:26-29

No belief is more central to Christianity than that this Teacher, Healer and Saviour was raised to life as 'Lord and God'. As the great Oxford don, C. S. Lewis, once said of his own move from atheism to Christian faith:

A man who was merely a man and said the sort of things Jesus said would not be a great moral teacher. He would either be a lunatic—on the level with a man who says he is a poached egg—or else he would be the Devil of Hell. You must make your choice. You can shut Him up for a fool, you can spit at Him and kill Him as a demon; or you can fall at His feet and call Him Lord and God. But let us not come with any patronising nonsense about His being a great human teacher. He has not left that open to us. He did not intend to.[7]

C.S. LEWIS

If the death of Jesus provides Christians with a robust self-esteem—knowing they are pardoned by the Almighty despite their many faults—Jesus' resurrection provides Christians with a deep confidence that their life and work in Christ's name is not in vain.[8]

Whether it is a missionary preaching Christ in a foreign country or Christian students, doctors, builders or footballers just trying to love God and other people from day to day, Christians live and speak as those who have glimpsed behind heaven's veil and have seen who really is in charge. It isn't politicians, pop stars, academics or the media; it is the one Thomas called 'My Lord and my God'. Knowing this, Christians invite the world to come and see for themselves that the God of universal conviction has come close to us in Jesus Christ.

PORTRAIT OF A CHRISTIAN

The God of common conviction has opened up his Kingdom to us in a tangible way in Jesus Christ. Christians seek to live in the light of this.

Christians believe that Christ's healings provide a glimpse of the restoration of all things in God's coming Kingdom. They see in Jesus' teaching, especially in his call to love God and neighbour, the shape of an authentic human life. They revere Christ as the one entrusted with God's final judgments and they rely on him as the one who died so that we might be freely forgiven. Above all, Christians believe that Jesus' resurrection establishes him as the divinely appointed Lord.

When asked by his followers how to speak to God, Jesus taught them the *Lord's Prayer* or *Our Father*. It is a beautiful expression of trust in God, a plea for forgiveness from God, a request that the Kingdom of God would shape our life here and now. In other words, it embodies the Christian worldview and serves as a constant reminder to the faithful that life and breath, judgment and mercy, work and play, the present and the future all belong to the One they are privileged to call the 'Father':

> Our Father in heaven,
> Hallowed (honoured) be your name.
> Your Kingdom come.
> Your will be done
>   on earth as it is in heaven.
> Give us today our daily bread.
> Forgive us our sins
>   as we forgive those who sin against us.
> Lead us not into temptation
>   but deliver us from evil.
> For the Kingdom, the power and the glory
>   are yours now and forever.
>   Amen.[9]

Modernity means ... that men (sic) take
control over the world and over themselves.
*What previously was experienced as fate now
becomes an arena of choices.* In principle, there
is the assumption that all human problems
can be converted into technical problems, and
if the techniques to solve certain problems
do not as yet exist, then they will have to
be invented. The world becomes ever more
"makeable."[1]

PETER L. BERGER

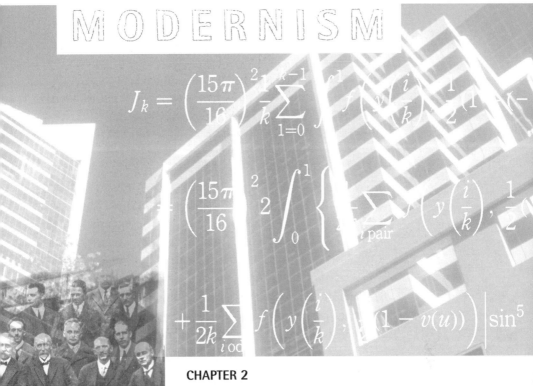

MODERNISM

$$J_k = \left(\frac{15\pi}{16}\right)^2 \frac{1}{k} \sum_{1=0}^{k-1} f\left(y\left(\frac{i}{k}\right)\right) \frac{1}{2}(1-$$

$$= \left(\frac{15\pi}{16}\right)^2 \frac{1}{2} \int_0^1 \left\{ \sum_{i\,pair} \left(y\left(\frac{i}{k}\right), \frac{1}{2}\right) \right.$$

$$+ \frac{1}{2k} \sum_{i\,oc} f\left(y\left(\frac{i}{k}\right), (1-v(u))\right) \right| \sin^5$$

CHAPTER 2

We have the technology

MODERNISM

Kirsten Birkett

INTRODUCTION

Cutler Beckett is the smarmy official of the East India Trading Company in the movie 'Pirates of the Caribbean: Dead man's chest'. As the movie opens, Beckett has arrested Will Turner and Elizabeth Swann (Orlando Bloom and Keira Knightley), who are sentenced to death for aiding Jack Sparrow's escape. On his swashbuckling adventures, Sparrow (played by Johnny Depp) is pitted against Beckett, who seeks to control the seas and put an end to pirates forever.

Beckett makes for an interesting character study. He is a man of modernism. He lives in the eighteenth century when technology and trade are conquering the world. There will no longer be blank spaces on the map, because ships can go anywhere. There are

> Jack Sparrow is a dying breed. The world is shrinking, the blank pages of the map filled in. Jack must find his place in the new world or perish.
>
> LORD CUTLER BECKETT IN 'PIRATES OF THE CARIBBEAN: DEAD MAN'S CHEST' MOTION PICTURE, 2006.

no mysterious depths labelled 'here be dragons', because men of science can go there and prove that there *are* no dragons. Science is starting to prove its value, technology is giving humans power over the forces of nature, and Europeans are beginning to think they can do just about anything.

Of course, as movie-viewers we know that Johnny Depp and Keira Knightley are going to prove that the magical, romantic way of living is best. But in reality it was the Cutler Beckett types who won out, while the pirates and their legends faded away. From the eighteenth century onwards, the blank pages of the map *were* filled in. Industry and technology *did* conquer the world. It was an incredible demonstration of the power that humans can have over their environment, and it came about because of a way of looking at the world that is known as 'modernism'.

SO WHAT IS MODERNISM?

If you study history, you might notice that Western history is typically divided into convenient categories. We have medieval, early modern, modern, and now postmodern. (You'll notice that historians generally don't use value-laden terms like 'Dark Ages' or 'Renaissance' any more. That is because we don't want to impose our value judgments on a period in history. That change in itself is rather postmodern.)

In political terms, the modern age is sometimes spoken of as the period between the fall of the Bastille in 1789 and the fall of the Berlin Wall in 1989. The French Revolution, the starting point of the modern age, is taken as the ultimate symbol of the Enlightenment, another word for the same era. (It's also known as the Age of Reason.) In the French Revolution, old loyalties to feudal lords, the power of the church, and the degeneracy and corrupt power of the aristocracy all gave way to liberty, equality, and the brotherhood of man. That was the theory; what really happened in the French revolution is another story. As an end point to the modern era, the Berlin Wall coming down symbolised the fall of one of the most powerful modernist systems, Marxism.

More than that, however, modernism can be thought of as a movement in the history of *ideas*; a way of thinking about humanity and the world that defined the end of the Middle Ages. This makes it harder to put dates on; ideas do not stop and start just when we want them to. Roughly, the modern era in the history of thought stretches from early modern— say, sixteenth and seventeenth centuries—until the twentieth century. It was characterised by various ideals.[2]

Modernism did not just stop; most people, actually, still believe the same ideals that modernists promoted. Many people are still modernists at heart, but express things these days in a postmodern sort of way. Other people might be postmodern in what they say but modern in how they live. People are like that—they use a mixture of ideas to make sense of whatever they're doing at the time. It might not be consistent, but it's very common.

Contact (Motion Picture) 1997

Jodie Foster's character in *Contact* is a modernist. She doesn't believe in God because she's a scientist, and says she has to go with the evidence, what she can prove. But when another character asks her to prove that her father loved her, she's stumped—because she hasn't realised that there are different kinds of evidence for different kinds of claims.

movies

HISTORY

science

Science without religion is lame; religion without science is blind.

ALBERT EINSTEIN

One of the major developments of the era, and in many ways the symbol of modernism, was science. It was the great success story of mankind and the icon of progress. It gave certainties and surety. In many ways, science stands for modernism.

It's difficult to put a starting date on the scientific revolution—you can trace it back as far as you like—but in Europe there was an outburst of new theories and a new movement away from medieval thinking around the sixteenth century. In the scholarly world, men such as Erasmus and Sir Thomas Moore made humanism a significant movement. In religion, the Reformation, when many countries broke away from the authority of the Pope and Rome, transformed doctrine as well as creating political turmoil. In what we would call science, or natural philosophy, 1543 was a big year. This was the date of the publication of Copernicus' *On the revolution of the heavenly spheres*, in which he suggested that the sun was at the centre of the universe with the planets going around it. In the same year, Harvey proposed his theory of the circulation of the blood; and Vesalius published a new book of anatomical drawings. These ideas were slow to take hold, and it wasn't until the next century that the scientific revolution could really be said to have happened.[3]

In England, early in the sixteen hundreds, a new methodology of learning was proposed by Francis Bacon.[4] It was *empiricist*; that is, he looked for knowledge in the world of experience; hard, objective facts. Previously, many people thought that what Aristotle and other ancient writers had said was good enough for anyone; they saw no need to test their theories against actual data. Bacon's very ambitious program was to collect immense amounts of factual data, then work out general laws from the data. Then, in turn, consequences could be deduced from the general laws and tested against data. You can see there the basis of what most people think of as the scientific method.

The scientific revolution in England really got going in the late seventeenth century, when the Royal Society of London was formed. Gentlemen would get together to demonstrate experiments and discuss natural philosophy, and many of them did serious scientific work at home, too. The Royal Society was consciously modelled on the philosophy of Francis Bacon.[5] They were going to draw their conclusions from experiment; the data came first, and was the foundation of all knowledge. They were testing the objective world, discovering hard data, and only then developing theories of explanation. Every theory would in turn be rigorously tested against the real world. The Society was remarkably successful. Isaac Newton matched the new astronomy with the mathematics to explain it. There was immense confidence about man's ability to discover the solutions to the physical problems of the world. Everything had a cause, and with enough effort and experiment, men of science could discover what it was.

In France, another famous figure had been working on the problem of knowledge; philosopher Rene Descartes. He was in search of knowledge you could be absolutely certain of. His system, however, was not experimental in the same way as the English natural philosophers. That is, he sought knowledge through the processes of thought. He set out to doubt everything he could, so he could throw away any knowledge that was not certain. This included doubting his existence. (Basically he was trying to question how we can know anything at all.) In this way he came to what he thought was a completely indisputable, certain fact; that *he existed*. He thought it was certain because if he doubted it, someone had to be doing the doubting, so he must exist; I think, therefore I am. He then 'proved' the existence of God, and God became the guarantor of all other certain knowledge that could be discovered. From these certain principles he deduced physical laws and so on. Descartes still did experiments; it was not all in his head, but he was determined to make sure that his thoughts were absolutely beyond doubt.[6]

As it turned out, a lot of the physics that Descartes did wasn't all that successful. He concluded, for instance, that it was impossible for there to be a vacuum in space. So the method was not entirely reliable as a practical tool for things like science.

The basic idea of modernism was that people believed science could solve most problems, and that with that tool humanity could understand all of reality.[7] The modern era was an immensely optimistic time. Intellectually, people could be sure about what was true; scientifically, knowledge would grow all the time; socially, technology would conquer illness, there would be growing prosperity; in all, humanity was progressing triumphantly. The world was expanding; more exploration was taking place, and new countries and civilisations were being discovered all the time. This was seen as a triumph for the countries that 'discovered' them. These countries, by right of discovery, belonged to the colonial power, and increased its wealth and prestige. It was not such good news for those being conquered and subjugated—something postmodernists rightly remind us of. Western man was dominating the world and there was no reason to think that he would not continue to do so.

It was an optimism based on a strong feeling of *certainty*. The use of reason and experiment, the two main systems about how to reach certain knowledge, were both *foundationalist*. That is, they both started from certain knowledge, whether it was empirical fact or self-evident truths. There were things you could know for sure, through the experimental method of science and the exercise of your own reason. These foundational truths were certain for everyone and for all time, and would give mankind a great deal of power.

Human reason and naturalistic principles began to triumph over the old, archaic systems of power. Revolutionaries such as Voltaire and Rosseau in France, and Thomas Paine, Thomas Jefferson and Benjamin Franklin in America, wrote treatises about the rights of man (women would come later) with a confidence in the future, and in the ability of political reform to solve problems. The title of Thomas Paine's book, *The Age of Reason*, sums it all up.[8]

What did modernism mean for religion?

In the early modern period, during the scientific revolution, God was definitely part of the picture. The Royal Society stated that it wished to demonstrate the 'power and wisdom, and goodness of the Creator, as it is displayed in the admirable order, and workmanship of the Creatures.' Indeed this kind of statement is very common in scientific writing of the time. Robert Boyle, for instance, seems to have been entirely genuine that his motivation for doing science was the glory of God. Isaac Newton included God in his cosmology.

What is frequently overlooked is the contribution that the Christian worldview played in the development of modern science. Professor Rodney Stark argues that the origin of science lay in monotheism and concluded 'science could only arise in a culture dominated by belief in a conscious, rational, all-powerful creator.'[10] Stark's argument is that medieval scholars laid down a base of belief in an orderly universe created by an orderly God—a system of thought that provided the impetus for the search for physical theories of an ordered universe; the quest to describe it mathematically and strive

I had no idea that the men whose science I used day by day – Newton, Pascal, Leibnitz, and Boyle for example ... were among a galaxy of scientists who had a conviction of God's existence that resulted in a dedication of their lives to him.[10]

PROFESSOR ROY E. PEACOCK

to map these laws of the physical world.[11] Stark points out that of 52 noted scientific pioneers of the sixteenth to eighteenth centuries, more than half were strong believers in Christian faith, and less than four percent were religious sceptics. It is ironic that today many people believe that science and religion are naturally opposed to one another.

Gradually, however, in the story of modernism a problem began to appear. Part of demonstrating God's power in nature was showing what a perfect machine it all was; but if the machine runs perfectly well on its own, where is the need for God? Also as the eighteenth century went on, the social issues, such as resentment of clerical power (especially in France), coloured the debate. The intellectuals resented the political power that the church had, and wanted to see it cut down. It was no accident that the French Revolution was against the church as well as the aristocracy.

movies

Pirates of the Caribbean (Motion picture) 2006

The swashbuckling adventure demonstrates our frustration with modernism. The 'point' of the movie is to demonstrate that modernism was wrong; that magic and superstition were real, and also much more exciting and valuable than nasty moneymaking modernism.

But in history, most would agree humans actually were much better off doing away with magic and superstition; the Enlightenment was actually a good thing. It's just that in doing away with everything supernatural it went too far, and removed a vital aspect of humanity and life—our spiritual realities.

So philosophically, a new kind of religion known as deism became more popular. In this system, God was gradually pushed away from his world. He was still there, as creator, but distant. He was not necessarily knowable. He did not intervene directly. Doubt was cast on miracles; they seemed a bit superstitious, a bit too supernatural. Since human reason and rationality were so important—and so demonstrably successful up to that stage—they became the criteria for religion. It was thought irrational to depend on revelation, with its supernaturalism. The best religion, it was thought, is that which can be deduced from nature alone. It was a natural religion, which consisted mainly of morality.[12]

Another development of modernism was the advances in historical criticism of the Bible. The philosopher David Hume had argued against the authenticity of miracles fairly early on. He said that a miracle was a very improbable event, by any standards of rationality. But since we know that humans are gullible and likely to be deceived, it is always more probable to assume that the witnesses were wrong, than that a miracle really happened. (This means that you don't actually have to examine the evidence at all; whatever it is, it's probably wrong).[13]

Around the middle of the eighteenth century publications began to appear which questioned the reliability of scripture. On the whole it was a sceptical movement, aiming to discredit the notion of scripture as inspired by God. In the late eighteenth and early nineteenth centuries historians became more self-consciously critical about their methods for reconstructing the past. This is not in itself a bad thing, but it was applied particularly ruthlessly to the Bible. The New Testament documents began to be described as 'myth'. This was not to say they were false, for people still believed that important religious truths were expressed, but thought that the gospels had to be divested of their 'mythical' elements. (More recent historical scholarship has overthrown much of what they said; the doubt they threw on the biblical documents for the most part was not valid. However, that point is not often emphasised in modern secular circles.)[14]

As science grew in popularity and power; as deists extolled the power of human reason above a superstitious dependence on revelation; as rationalists complained that the church had too much political power; biblical religion began to suffer. The specific historical attacks on the Scriptures shook people's confidence in them. At the same time, science was held up as an alternative way to understand the world. Reason was regarded as much more reliable than revelation, and the historical research into the Scriptures only appeared to confirm this. Biblical Christianity suffered many attacks.

It would be easy to conclude that the Enlightenment was a time when Christianity was dead, either weak or overthrown altogether. Certainly that is the impression many writers give. In simplistic terms, reason overtook God, and God was pushed aside. This was not the whole story, however; after all, the eighteenth century was also the time of the evangelical awakening in England, which is regarded as one of the highpoints of church history. The Wesleys and their followers evangelised the whole country and a massive Christian movement was begun. It was also the time of the great revivals in America. Preachers like Jonathon Edwards are still held up as heroes in evangelical Christian circles. A great ground swell of religion swept America.

Also, for a lot of people science was still used as a vehicle for explaining God's power and foresight. William Paley's *Natural Theology*, one long argument from design, was written in 1802 and was immensely popular. Science was not always seen as the enemy of Christianity. A very large proportion of practising scientists in England were clergy.

Even so, where the early modern period saw science as the exploration of the glory of God, by the late nineteenth century this rational process had excluded religious ideas from the category of things that it is possible to know rationally. Instead, religion was thought of as mere opinion. The philosopher Immanuel Kant claimed that God was in himself unknowable and unprovable. Many people hold this view today.

So that is modernism; belief in the power of the human mind to discover objective truth, and solve human problems on earth. Modernism claims that if we have the right starting point, and the right method, we can pretty much solve any problem. Humankind is progressing and life is improving. There *is* a right perspective to have on life and the makeup of our world, and we are capable of discovering it by the process of reason.

CENTRAL BELIEFS

We could summarise some of the key features of modernism as follows:

1. It focuses on humans. It carries within it great confidence in humans being able to use reason to create meaning and significance for themselves.

2. It argues that we can and should seek to know things for certain.

3. It tends towards naturalist thinking or belief in a closed universe ie. no intervention from outside the universe from any god or spiritual power. At the very least there is enormous scepticism regarding the supernatural. The natural world is all there is.

4. It claims that the trick to understanding any area of life properly is to get the basic principles—the foundation—right.

5. Modernism is characterised by a striving for control over the world through rational-technical means.[15]

6. It focuses on ascertaining appropriate methods. Knowing how to go about understanding the world is the key to getting that understanding right. Modernism champions science and the experimental method.

7. It is commitedto the idea that what is true here and now is true everywhere, at every time.[16]

8. Through an inflated sense of the potential for human agents to control the world, many aspects of modern political, social and cultural life are thoroughly secularised (not regarded as religious, spiritual or sacred).[17]

SCEPTICS

'It's hard for me to believe that everything out there is just an accident ... [Yet] I don't have any religious belief. I don't believe that there is a God. I don't believe in Christianity, or Judaism or anything like that, OK? I'm not an atheist ... I'm not an agnostic. ... I'm just in a simple state. I don't know what there is or might be ... But on the other hand, what I can say is that it seems likely to me that this particular universe we have is the consequence of something which I would call intelligent.'

PHYSICIST EDWARD FRIEDKIN[18]

IMPACT

Modernism changed the Western world, and basically created the world of science and technology. People were hugely enthusiastic, and optimistic about the future. Think about what came out of the 'Age of Reason'—steam engines, industrial machines, factories, fast travel, instant international communication, trains, cars, air travel, penicillin, anaesthetics—and that only takes us to the early twentieth century! It's no wonder that people thought human ingenuity could solve all the world's problems. It must have seemed as if suddenly all the old barriers to human progress were being overcome.

One of the most significant ways in which this affected society was the power it gave to science. Science was solving problems; science was giving the answers. It was a long time before people became aware that science and the technology it produced were also creating major problems (pollution, extinction of species, overuse of non-renewable resources, world-threatening weapons and so on). These are late twentieth-century realisations, for the most part. Until then, people were overwhelmed at the positive power of science, and it seemed that science was the answer to everything.

In many ways, people are wary of science these days. There is not the same respect for scientific pronouncements that there was, say, fifty years ago, when a man in a white coat could state that a washing powder worked and everyone believed it. It would appear that as a society we are more sceptical about the scientific endeavour. The devastation of two world wars, genocide in Germany and Rwanda, the atomic bomb and threat of nuclear devastation, and environmental degradation, have placed a huge dent in the confidence we once had in science and the modern project. Very significantly the failure of science and rationalism, on their own, to come up with compelling answers to the biggest questions of life such as where we find meaning and hope, has left us more cynical and questioning.

However we can still see the huge impact belief in science has on our society, particularly when it comes to God. Scientists are still seen in movies, on television documentaries and dramas, and in newspaper articles, as the rational, intelligent people who are most likely to be right. When it comes down to it, we still believe that science has the answers, in police work, in discovering aliens, in politics.

Modernism in action

Police dramas now focus on modern scientific methods of crime detection, tending to give much weight to the ability of evidence to get to the truth. Grissom on *CSI* is a thorough modernist. He thinks evidence never lies, and science can tell us the truth, always. In an episode of CSI the team of forensic police are on the case of a gang who have been responsible for attacking tourists just for the fun of it. Eventually a victim of these random assaults is beaten so badly, he dies. After solving the crime with their usual mix of scientific acumen and police instincts, Catherine explains that apart from the leader, the rest of the gang are all teenagers, apparently 'without a conscience'. Grissom believes that a culture of shamelessness is a contributing factor. 'A moral compass can only point you in the right direction, it can't make you go there', he says.

For a modernist like Grissom, what is it that would make someone follow a moral compass, pointing him or her 'in the right direction'?

CONTACT AND DEPARTURE FROM CHRISTIANITY

Christians agree with modernists in some ways, such as the belief that we *can* know truth about the world. The Bible says God wants us to know the truth, and he has created us capable of finding out truth—not just my view or your view, or some cultural perspective, but the real, objective truth. It's out there, and if we use our brains and senses and work at it, we can know something of reality.

Christians also agree with the scientific way of thinking. It's important to have reasons for what you believe. It's not good enough to accept a statement just on someone's say-so. We should test it out, investigate, find out if it's right and importantly, if it works. Christians are as enthusiastic as anyone else in applauding the use of logic and reason to produce life-enhancing technology. Christians can say 'amen' to most of the achievements of scientific endeavours, being glad we have modern dentistry, air travel, hygiene, drugs that prevent us dying of a common cold, developing polio or losing children in childbirth—even the microwave oven or home coffee machine. A Christian perspective would value the contribution of these things while acknowledging their limits.

Christianity does not trust human reason quite as absolutely as modernism. The Bible says that, while God created us with intelligence and rational minds, our personal bias can override our reason. Even the most intelligent of us, the Bible says, are quite capable of shutting our eyes to the evidence if it's not what we want to see. There is plenty of evidence for instance that material possessions and money do not provide lasting satisfaction (a strong biblical idea). But in our consumer-driven culture that is not what we want to hear, so we ignore the warnings and pursue material wealth at huge cost to relationships, health and community obligations.

Most of all, the Bible says, human beings can be entirely blind when it comes to thinking about God. While there are many good reasons for concluding that a god exists, the Bible says that humans will not want to accept the evidence—they would rather live as if there is no God. So the modernist wish to make religion 'rational' actually backfires, because this is one area where humans are anything but rational. Although it is entirely rational to believe in God (who, the Bible claims, came to earth in human form and left plenty of evidence of his existence and what he wants us to do about it), still any number of people put their faith in anything else rather than accept God.

The Christian is not rationalistic; he does not try to begin from himself autonomously and work out a system from there on. But he *is* rational; he thinks and acts on the basis that A is A and A is not non-A. However he does not end with only rationality, for in his response to what God has said his whole personality is involved.[21]

FRANCIS SCHAEFFER

Essentially Christian belief highlights the *limits* of science and rationalism in terms of addressing the really big questions of life—the worldview questions —'Who am I?'. 'Why am I here?', 'What is the purpose of existence?', 'Where are we going?', 'Where does hope lie?'. What does science really have to say about these things? When we consider humanity from a purely biological perspective and the universe in solely material terms there are gaping holes in understanding the fullness of life. There might be some value in examining the chemicals involved in someone feeling love for another person, or the genetic predisposition for belief in a spiritual world—but most of us resist being spoken of in such functional and reductionist language.

The Bible on the other hand, tells a story that is full and rich and speaks into every aspect of the human condition—including our origins, our identity, our place in the world, and where we are heading. Without science we would understand very little about our physical world and most of us would not survive to read this book. But science alone without reference to the transcendent, according to Christian understanding leaves us floundering before questions of meaning and purpose, without answers and without hope.

David Wells, writing of the change brought on by the Enlightenment says:

> The place God had occupied was now occupied by the human being. Meaning and morality, which only God could give, were taken to be purely human accomplishments; but in promising what only God could do, the Enlightenment sowed the seeds of its own downfall. It promised too much. It promised, in fact, that all human problems could be solved purely by natural means—and that, plainly, rested on false assumptions. [21]

RESPONSE

1. What would be a good slogan to sum up the underlying beliefs of modernism?

2. What is the significance of the fall of the Bastille and the fall of the Berlin Wall in measuring the age of modernism? Is the age of modernism truly over?

3. Which ten words would best characterise and describe the modern worldview?

DiSCUSSiON

A. Why might modernism be described as being naively optimistic?

B. In what ways might modernism and science be detrimental to a Christian worldview?

C. In what ways might modernism and science be supportive of a Christian worldview?

D. Is modernist scepticism regarding revelation and the supernatural still dominant in contemporary Western society? What does your experience tell you about this?

The story that we need

But in the end, science does not provide the answers most of us require. Its story of our origins and of our end is, to say the least, unsatisfactory. To the question, 'How did it all begin?' science answers, 'Probably by an accident'. To the question, 'How will it all end?', science answers, 'Probably by an accident'. And to many people, the accidental life is not worth living. Moreover, the science-god has no answer to the question, 'Why are we here?' and, to the question, 'What moral instructions do you give us?', the science-god maintains silence. It places itself at the service of both the beneficent and the cruel, and its grand moral impartiality, if not indifference, makes it, in the end, no god at all.[22]

NEIL POSTMAN

DiSCUSSiON

E. Does Neil Postman capture the modernist problem effectively? Do you agree with his assessment? What would be your own answers to each of the crucial questions he poses that he claims science is unable to answer satisfactorily?

Is it all in the genes?

Scientists have made extraordinary discoveries about the role that our genetic makeup plays in determining what we are like as people. Geneticists will explain that propensity to diseases, such as different cancers, heart disease, obesity, diabetes, kidney failure, arthritis, back pain, and many others is very largely determined by our genes. Some studies have found very significant links between genes and aspects of personality such as

IQ, fingerprints, how much money you are likely to make, your choice of career, choice of partner, even how much TV you watch. More controversial is the claim by some researchers that even the likelihood of belief in God has a genetic component to it.

There is little doubt genes play a huge role in the sort of people we become, and we should be grateful for many of the advances in medical technology due to gene research. Yet many of us recoil from the idea of being reduced merely to a bunch of chemicals coming together in cells in a particular way. The claim of a 'God gene'—not by any means an accepted reality—is an example of the way science can at times reduce life and reality to something much less than its totality. We protest that there must be more than this. As individuals we are so much more than what the scientist can describe; life and our experiences are greater than what can be explained using a test tube, microscope or CT scan, or even a study involving thousands of others.

DiSCUSSiON

F. Are there aspects of life where you feel science is limited and not able to tell us about?

G. What might these limitations tell us about the worldview that is modernist rationalist and closed to the transcendent?

PeRCEPTiON

1. What appear to you to be the key strengths of modernism as a way of viewing the world?

2. What are its most identifiable weaknesses?

CHAPTER 3

Blown away: POSTMODERNISM

Greg Clarke

INTRODUCTION:
EXPLODING A WORLDVIEW

On 15 July 1972, at 3.32pm someone blew up a building and postmodernism was born.

When it was first built, the Pruitt-Igoe housing project in St Louis, Missouri was hailed as a landmark of modern architecture. It stood as the epitome of modernity itself, since it employed state of the art technology to create an internally self-sufficient urban environment. A mini utopia; it was supposed to solve the problems of the urban poor by translating sophisticated social philosophy into a perfect physical space.

But the inhabitants hated it and used everything they could to resist this attempt at social engineering:

> If there are no absolutes in the objective realm, neither can there be absolutes in the subjective realm. There can be no fixed identity, no sense of self, no unified human soul. Modernism was activist, optimistic, and self-confident. Postmodernism is passive, cynical, and insecure.[1]
>
> GENE EDWARD
> VEITH, JNR

they vandalised it, covered it with graffiti, and ultimately destroyed it until the government gave up on the project and blew it up with dynamite.

This incident is a marvellous summary of the move from modernity to postmodernity, modernism to postmodernism. The modern sought control, perfection, progress, self-sufficiency, utopia. The postmodern rejected each of these elements—he (or she) blew them sky high.

CENTRAL BELIEFS

Postmodernism is a slippery term, but whatever it is, it's after modernism. If we are going to call something 'post', we can start to understand it by what it comes after. There are lots of ways you can sum up modernism, but basically it refers to the period of human history after the Enlightenment and the rapid development of industry, travel, communication and globalisation. We can point to six keys to modernism:

1. It is human-centred.

2. It argues that we can and should seek to know things for certain.

3. It claims that the trick to understanding any area of life properly is to get the basic principles—the foundation—right.

4. It champions science and the experimental method.

5. The natural world is all there is.

6. It exhibits a profound commitment to ahistorical universality—what is true here and now is true everywhere, at every time.

Adjectives that apply to modernism include: solid, rational, systematic, progressive, controlled, better.

Let's picture a garden-variety modernist. He is a firm believer that science has rid us of the need for belief in God. The laws of nature will eventually explain all of life's complexities. He sees the human race as making progress, finding cures for diseases, building better housing and increasing our grasp on how the world operates. He is confident that what is right for him is right for everybody, and people would all get on better if they could stick to the basic rules of morality and civilisation.

This kind of person is becoming increasingly rare in the twenty-first century. Very few people believe that what is right for one individual will necessarily be right for all. Although we are making progress in areas such as medicine and civil services, most people these days doubt that we will ever rid the world of AIDS, cancer, malnutrition and any number of other afflictions. People tend to think that life is more complex and mysterious than we will ever fathom.

The views expressed in the previous paragraph are likely to come from the mouth of a 'postmodernist'. This individual has encountered the modernist viewpoint and found it lacking. The postmodernist (or postmodern, which is the usual short-hand) will have objections to the statements the modernist made, objections which, respectively, look something like this:

1. I am unsure of my own opinions and identity.

2. I don't think we can know anything for certain. In fact, it is arrogant to even try to do so.

3. The basic principles of life are hard to discover, and may not be discoverable. Perhaps there aren't any basic principles; perhaps everyone thinks about it differently.

4. Everyone has different methods of understanding, and no-one can say one is

better than another. Science is one good method, but even it isn't fail-safe. Perhaps less rational approaches to life should be used too.

5. Although this world is probably all there is, no-one can be sure.

6. What's right for me may not be right for you. Make up your own mind about what is true.

Adjectives that might be applied to postmodernism include: liquid, thoughtful, provisional, complex, random, relative.

From comparing these two lists of features, we can see that postmodernism is the **result** of modernism, and also the **rejection** of modernism.

HISTORY

Historically, the path from modernism to postmodernism passes through two World Wars, with all of their chaos and hopelessness. The wars challenged the notion that humanity could 'better' itself through ideology, science, technology and progress—instead, the evidence suggested that with all our knowledge and desire for advancement, in fact we had made things worse. Intellectuals began to reflect on the kinds of ideas that had led to the wars, and to reject them one-by-one.

Most of the key figures in the discussion of postmodernism are European, with the most influential hailing from France. It may be that postmodern thinking is somehow linked with French culture, but that is not to say that it hasn't caught on in many other parts of the world.

Like most 'isms', the engine room of postmodernism is the philosophy department. The writings of the philosophers form the backdrop for much of the cultural change that we now call postmodernism. Let's consider three key figures and their major contributions.

Jean-Francois Lyotard

Lyotard, a French philosopher, was commissioned in the 1970s to write a report about knowledge for the Quebec government. His resulting 1979 book, *La Condition postmoderne* (*The Postmodern Condition*) made him famous. One of his key observations was that what we consider to be true knowledge is shaped by certain 'big stories' that we accept about the world. These big stories give us a set of rules and principles by which we understand everything else. Lyotard described these stories as 'metanarratives' and concluded that in the late twentieth century, these metanarratives were less and less acceptable. People started to think that metanarratives were simply used politically and culturally as instruments of power for controlling knowledge. Lyotard wrote that in our postmodern age, we have *a suspicion towards metanarratives*, by which he meant that people are edgy about whether there is a 'big story' that helps us to understand all the other stories. As Homer Simpson says at the end of an episode of *The Simpsons*, when the characters are trying to tie together all the elements of the story, 'Maybe it's just a bunch of stuff that happened'. In other words, the question is raised: is there any over-arching, all-encompassing piece of knowledge that helps us grasp the rest of it? Drawing on thinkers like Lyotard, postmoderns tend to say, 'We suspect not'.

SUBJECTIVISM

A helpful aspect of postmodern theory has been to recognise that all human perception emerges out of a particular point of view, and therefore has a subjective element to it (the extreme postmodern would say it is entirely subjective!). This point of view is not only affected by 'where you are sitting' or the particular time and place in which a person lives and operates, but 'who you are' or the way in which the person doing the viewing is impacted by his or her own race, sex, class, education, mental health, family background, and personality ethnicity. These are all shaping factors in how individuals will perceive the world around them.[2]

Postmodernism therefore has a deep scepticism regarding the comprehensive systems and the 'right' or correct way of doing things. The postmodern will be suspicious or will reject outright any notion of the 'correct' way of painting a picture, educating a child, or building a building.[3]

Jacques Derrida

A major philosopher of our times is the Algerian Jewish man, Jacques Derrida, who died in 2004 at the age of 74. He was a brilliant scholar, and very ambitious – his work set out to redirect the course of philosophy, and went some way towards doing just that.

Derrida wrote difficult, playful sentences, often using three languages, and often writing about little known authors and obscure ideas. But Derrida was trying to get his readers to *think twice* about what they thought they knew, and his writing style was part of that.

Derrida worked at what he called 'deconstruction'— pulling apart a text and showing where there are holes in the reasoning. Derrida didn't describe his work as postmodern, but this activity of deconstruction is an important part of postmodern life. One major implication of Derrida's work is the idea that it is difficult, perhaps impossible, for written words to 'get at' the truth. The truth is never present; it is always absent. There will always be something in our attempts to express the truth that can be deconstructed to show that they don't simply mean what we think they mean. An example of this problem is the line in the American Declaration of Independence, that 'all men are created equal'. At the time it was written, the word 'man' meant something like 'humanity' or 'all human beings', but we can deconstruct that sentence to show that by using the gender-specific term 'man', the sentence doesn't really say today what it seems to say on first look. It is a simplistic example to help us grasp the idea of deconstructing—it points out the 'gaps' in our understanding and shows that meanings shift over time and cultures.

In his later life, Derrida became very interested in ethics and social questions: How can people forgive each other for things like war atrocities? What is friendship? Can we speak of justice? These might seem like unusual questions for a postmodern philosopher, but they indicate where postmodern thinking leads people: not to nihilism and the loss of all values, but to a reconsideration of values that were merely assumed to be true.

Michel Foucault

Foucault was born in 1926 in Poitiers, France. He was very influenced by the German philosopher, Friedrich Nietzsche, who taught that behind every idea there was a set of 'powers' at work, trying to influence and manipulate people. Foucault explored the ways in which society's institutions have been set up to give power to some people and deprive it from others. For example, he studied the way mental hospitals and prisons were set up to give power to the doctors and guards, and take it away from the patients and prisoners. Foucault saw in these institutions a microcosm of how the whole of modern civilisation operated—some people and some ideas are considered 'safe' and 'right', while others are considered 'dangerous' and 'deviant'.

One of Foucault's main ideas was that knowledge is closely related to power. He taught that what we consider true is not simply something that is the case for everyone at all times (what we described above as 'ahistorical universality'). Rather, 'truth' is constructed out of a certain set of circumstances and a certain set of preconceived ideas. It is also always serving a political or social service—truth is always giving power and authority to someone over someone else.

Growing up Roman Catholic and gay, Foucault's unhappiness led him on a search to escape the self and to live only for pleasure. Foucault's efforts to 'get away' from himself were an outworking of his belief that humanity had accepted a faulty and misguided interest in the autonomy of the human being. Our 'self', for Foucault, was a form of pride, of thinking we had control over the world when in fact we do not. Foucault traced this view back to the Enlightenment, to the time of enormous confidence in reason and science and the human ability to conquer the world. As a postmodern, Foucault wanted to get beyond this arrogant view.

In summary, Foucault found truth to be constructed and politically motivated, human nature to be impossible to define, human behaviour to be controlled by our need for power and pleasure, and religion to be merely the codification of all of these things.

THE SELF AS VILLAGE MARKETPLACE

A classroom university lecture on the neuroscientist José Delgado by a character in Tom Wolfe's novel, *I am Charlotte Simmons*, allows Wolfe to present the following argument:

'[N]ot only emotions but also purpose and intentions are physical matters. ... [Delgado's] position was that the human mind, as we conceive it—and I think all of us do—bears very little resemblance to reality. We think of the mind—we can't help but think of the mind—as something from a command centre in the brain, which we call the 'self', and that this self has free will. Delgado called that a 'useful illusion'. He said there was a whole series of neural circuits ... that work in parallel to create the illusion of a self—'me', an 'individual' with free will and a soul. He called the self nothing more than a 'transient composite of materials from the environment'. It's not a command centre but a village marketplace, an arcade, or a lobby, like a hotel lobby, and other people and their ideas and their mental atmosphere and the Zeitgeist—the spirit of the age, to use Hegel's term from 200 years ago—can come walking right on in, and you can't lock the doors, because they become you, because they are you. After Delgado, neuroscientists began to put the words self and mind and, of course, soul in quotation marks.'[4]

IMPACT

These ideas from the field of philosophy have had a powerful impact in other fields. They have 'trickled down' into disciplines like literature—sometimes 'exploded on to the stage' would be a better way of describing their influence.

In the field of **ethics**, postmodernism has shifted the focus from asking questions about what is right and what ought to take place, to questions about what communities agree upon as standards of behaviour, and using what *is* taking place as a guide to what is permissible for society. For example, the ratings given to literature and film (PG, M, R, etc) are assessed according to what a community deems acceptable, not according to a set of solid morals or ethical absolutes. Postmoderns are very interested in ethics, but wish to answer ethical questions without referring to a set of transcendent or everlasting virtues.

In **architecture**, areas such as Melbourne's Federation Square precinct are often described as postmodern. Designed to display 'difference with coherence', the assortment of buildings and sculptures appears fragmented, perhaps unstable, and certainly confusing—and yet it somehow holds together. It challenges the idea that symmetry is required for order (although, architects admit

Modernist confidence in human autonomy could be summed up as 'We can find out what we need to find out, in order to think what we need to think, in order to do what we need to do, in order to get what we want to get.'

It is this confidence that has been lost in postmodernism. [5]

JOHN G. STACKHOUSE JNR.

FEDERATION SQUARE, MELBOURNE

there is still a basic need for mathematical order to stop these buildings falling over!). There is a great playfulness to postmodern architecture, and pleasure in mixing together styles and materials that are often thought incompatible, such as classical formality and contemporary plastics.

In **literature**, postmodern writing usually defies the expectations of a particular genre. If it is a novel, where we expect a beginning, middle and end, this may be denied us. For example, James Joyce's novel *Finnegan's Wake* (written at the beginning of the twentieth century, but setting the pace for postmodern writing) begins in the middle of a sentence, which is completed at the novel's close. Postmodern literature is often lacking in seriousness of tone, even when the content is tragic or deeply thoughtful; this playfulness is an outcome of the suspicion among postmoderns that we can arrive at final meanings. Instead of despairing of such a situation, postmoderns throw back their heads and celebrate with abandon. Postmodern writing is often quirky and mysterious. One writer, Georges Perec, wrote a novel without using the letter 'e' in any of its words. Why? Who knows? Because he could; just for the fun of it.

In **film**, we see the influence of postmodernism at the levels of story and technique. Many films of the past few decades have storylines in which the 'truth' is hard to find. Take, for example, *The Matrix*. Is Neo really part of another world, a matrix beyond normal perception? Does he know who he is, or does he have little understanding of his true identity? Can he trust Morpheus, or Agent Smith, or anyone he encounters? Does he rule over technology or does it rule over him? This level of uncertainty is a distinguishing feature of postmodern culture.

movies

Pulp Fiction (Motion Picture) 1994

Quentin Tarantino's 1994 cult classic *Pulp Fiction* contains many of the elements of filmmaking we could describe as postmodern. Starring John Travolta, Samuel L. Jackson, Bruce Willis, and Uma Thurman, the film draws together a series of disparate stories linked by bizarre circumstances.

Typical of the postmodern genre, the film plays with a non-linear storyline—the opening scene of the film also becomes the final scene, and even that is not in chronological order. Scenes include juxtaposing grave, serious subject matter —two hitmen about to carry out an execution—with frivolous discussion about French names for McDonalds hamburgers. One of the hitmen, Jules (Samuel L. Jackson) is something of a closet philosopher and quotes from the Bible before shooting his hapless victims.

The film merges drama, comedy and action in a manner that defies convention. A massive hit, the film inspired many other films that followed it in embracing the postmodern spirit of the age.

Visual and filmic techniques that might be described as ways of expressing postmodern notions include pastiche (a collection of incongruous elements), non-linear narratives (story-lines that don't follow the normal flow of time and events) and visual allusion (for example, in presenting a scene the point is to remind us of a scene from another movie—*The Simpsons* does this all the time).

Generally, the field of **entertainment** tells us a lot about the way postmoderns think. There is a great emphasis on the visual, often trumping the verbal. This is partly a result of the loss of confidence in words as conveyors of truth. There also has been a 'levelling out' of values in the arts, such that it is often claimed that there is no meaningful difference between 'high art' (painting, sculpture, classical music) and 'popular art' (comics, television, pop music). At high school Shakespeare's play, *Romeo and Juliet* is studied alongside film or comic book versions of the play, without any assessment of whether one form is truer, artistically greater or morally more valuable than another. Whereas in the modern era, it would have been assumed that the ancient and original voice of Shakespeare would take educational priority, in the postmodern context this is no longer assumed.

In **politics**, the influence of postmodernism is evident in what is called 'spin'. If a politician has a somewhat loosened approach to 'The Truth', thinking perhaps with Derrida that meaning is elusive and the truth is never quite present, then he or she will speak and write in whatever way best suits the cause. If this means using euphemisms, hiding facts, leaving out significant parts of a story, and coming up with catchphrases rather than substantial policies, well so be it. With Foucault, the politician knows that truth and power are related, and if what is said is *perceived* to be true (regardless of whether it is), he or she will be given the authority to lead us. 'Truth' gets defined as what you can convince others of.

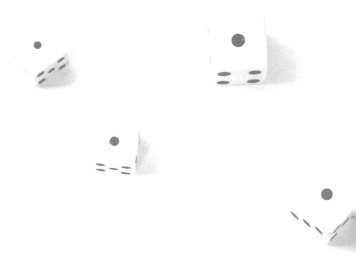

POSTMODERNISM ON THE STREET

Contemporary music uses old songs re-mixed with current rhythms and beats. This is largely a reflection of the postmodern penchant for slapping together disparate styles in an eclectic mix, a pastiche of unusual or humorous combinations, which has also been seen in art and architecture.

Modernist architecture tended towards a quest for unity and hence uniformity. The rectangular inverted shoebox skyscraper, typical of this quest, was picked up no more enthusiastically than in Stalinist Russia and Eastern Europe. Buildings there were relentlessly similar, functional and oppressive.

The postmodern reaction against such uniform structures has produced some refreshingly different buildings.

The Hundertwasser House in Vienna, Austria is an excellent example of postmodern architecture and art. The building defies conventions, having no right angles, and is packed with a mix of colours and styles. Large trees grow on the roof and from various balconies. There is an eclectic mix of tile, and brick façade; columns and steeples, church spires and colonnades. It represents a playful, artistic determination to be unpredictable, unique and diverse.

CONTACT AND DEPARTURE FROM CHRISTIANITY

We come now to think about postmodernism in relation to Christian beliefs. There is no simple equation that says 'postmodernism is compatible with Christianity', nor that 'Christianity and postmodernism are enemies'. We will need to think more carefully than that about the relationship between the religion of Jesus Christ and this movement of thought and culture that we are part of called postmodernism.

Let's consider postmodern claims in relation to four areas: knowledge, ethics, entertainment, and the future.

knowledge

Postmodern scepticism about human ability to know the truth has been considered a deep attack on Christianity. Christians believe that God can be known through Jesus Christ, in the words of the Bible, and postmodernism seems to be suggesting that a Christian could not be sure of this.

At one level, this is the case. Christians do believe that truth is found in Christ, while postmoderns insist that such truth is elusive and never really present. However, in another way, there is something to be said for the scepticism about knowledge that postmodernism suggests. It is sceptical that human beings *on their own* can be sure of the truth. This is quite compatible with the Christian idea that God reveals the truth to a person through the work of the Holy Spirit. Christianity is not found and accepted by deep reasoning and philosophy; it is found by God entering a person's heart and mind and convicting him or her.

Furthermore, the Christian faith is a kind of metanarrative, which sits uneasily with Lyotard's criticism of all such 'over-arching stories'. Christian faith is a big-scale interpretation of the world, history and where the world is headed. But once again, there is a truth in Lyotard's criticism; systems of thought that claim to tie up every loose end are built on human bravado, not on genuine knowledge. The Christian metanarrative has enough information in it about the world, history and the future to provide a confident guide to life, but it doesn't nail down every detail of life into an impenetrable system of thought. It is more humane than that!

Foucault's idea that the self is constructed sits uneasily with the Christian claim that human beings are created in God's image and find their worth in that special status as his creatures. But once again, something worthwhile can be salvaged from the postmodern wreck, because modernism had placed such an emphasis on the individual and on human ability that there is a kind of humility in the postmodern view that our selves are more fragile and need to be shaped. Christianity offers an explanation of who can do the shaping—God himself, through the Holy Spirit, shaping believers in conformity to the Lord Jesus.

ethics

Postmodern ethics is a quest to be good without God. It admits that there need to be guides and restrictions on human behaviour, and that human beings go off the rails and don't even live up to their own standards. There is some common ground between postmodern ethical concerns and Christian codes of behaviour, such as the commandments found in Scripture and Jesus' teachings in passages such as the Sermon on the Mount. Postmoderns are often interested in justice, in caring for marginalised people, in opposing greed and selfishness, and in challenging corrupt authorities. These behaviours match well with Christian ethics.

However, there is a fluidity and subjectiveness to postmodern ethics that is not in concord with the teachings of the Bible. There are clear teachings in Scripture concerning acceptable behaviour, and to suggest that these are uncertain or indeterminate is to stick your postmodern head in the sand. It is probably fair to generalise and say that in the area of social ethics, Christian worldview and postmodernism have some things in common, but in the areas of personal ethics they are a long way apart.

entertainment

Because of the postmodern emphasis on playfulness and reluctance to commit to notions of 'the Truth', this is an era of entertainment. Never before has so much time, so many resources and so much creative energy gone into entertaining ourselves. One scholar, Neil Postman, has described this activity as 'amusing ourselves to death'. Twenty-four hour television, video games, endless movies, junk food, sport, gimmicky plastic toys—these all have some connection to the postmodern idea that we are not here on a quest for truth, but just keeping ourselves occupied as best we can while death approaches.

Christians, in contrast, believe that God has given life a purpose, and it is found in worshipping and serving him. The Christian life is to be full of good works, thoughtful use of time and resources, and ongoing efforts to further the kingdom of the Lord Jesus. Some Christians could use a bit more 'play' in their lives—because true Christianity is never uptight and has plenty of room for relaxing and enjoying yourself. But, overall, there is an enormous contrast between the purposeful Christian life and the 'treading water gleefully while the ship sinks' postmodern philosophy.

STORIES ABOUT NOTHING

The long running television sit-com *Seinfeld* had a typically postmodern feel in its determination to focus on the trivial. The whole notion that undergirded the program was 'a story about nothing'. Each of the characters, Jerry, Elaine, George and Kramer, appeared to be outdoing each other in who could be more superficial and shallow. It could be said to be postmodern in reacting against trying to be of any substance or to stand for anything other than entertainment.

By contrast the 1970s comedy *M*A*S*H*, set in an American Army field hospital during the Korean War, is a 'modern' example of a comedy that nonetheless aimed to comment on society and human relationships, with an especially anti-war theme running throughout its 200 plus episodes.[6]

the future

Just as postmodernism results in a sense of purposelessness about life, so it has little to offer when it comes to the future. It does not see a point to history, as if human life were headed somewhere, or the universe itself served some great end. All that awaits us is darkness. While postmodernism enjoys the benefits of human progress, it is also aware of their costs. Wonderful drugs are developed to stave off disease, but they cost millions of dollars that might have gone to save unnecessarily ill children in poor countries. Large cities may provide us with 24/7 access to any modern conveniences we desire, but that comes at the expense of the breakdown of family togetherness and the isolation of many 'urban orphans', the over-stretching of transport resources, and incredible amounts of planet-destroying pollution. There is some sense of hope in postmodernism—hope for a future that is liberated from oppressive systems of thought and moral control—but it is a fleeting and misty hope. Derrida leaves the door open in his thought for the possibility that there could be salvation around the corner for humanity, but he doesn't wait up expectantly to see who arrives.

The Christian view of the future, in contrast, is very confident. It is built on the understanding that Jesus Christ is the key to history—past, present, future—and that his death and resurrection have fulfilled God's plans for the world and ushered in already the kingdom of God. Christians believe that we now live in the time of the Spirit, when God is making on earth a dwelling place where he can live with humanity in peace and holiness. While all the details of this future have not been made known, its security is undoubted, because it has already begun. The Christian gospel challenges postmodernism at this point, head to head, offering a meaningful interpretation of what this life is all about, and one that can listen carefully to the critiques of knowledge and ethics that postmodernism offers, and be all the better for it.

RESPONSE

QUeST¿ON

1. What would be a good slogan to sum up the underlying beliefs of postmodernism?

2. What do you suppose have been the main factors in disillusionment with modernism?

3. Identify as many specific influences of postmodernism on our culture as you can think of. Think of advertisements, music, film, the way people speak, ideas of right and wrong, specific architectural structures.

DiSCUSSiON

A. 'While we might have all been influenced by postmodernism, most people in our culture are really modernists.' What aspects of your own view of the world are modern/postmodern?

B. Arthur Croker, himself a postmodernist, says the key psychological mood of this postmodern culture is panic, a 'free fall' that comes from 'the disappearance of external standards of public conduct ... and the dissolution of internal foundations of identity.'[7]

   Where do you see 'panic' in our culture? Do you agree with Croker's assessment of the impact of postmodernism on the psyche of the culture?

I'm so postmodern

The Bedroom Philosopher, *In Bed With My Doona* (Album)

I'm so postmodern that I just don't talk anymore,
I wear different coloured t-shirts according to my mood.
I'm so postmodern that I work from home as a surf life saving consumer
    hotline.
I'm so postmodern that all my clothes are made out of sleeping bags,
I don't need pockets, I'm a pocket myself.
I'm so postmodern I go to parties I'm not invited to and locate the vegemite
    and write my name on everyone.
I'm so postmodern that I write reviews for funerals, and heckle at
    weddings from inside a suitcase.
I'm so postmodern I'm going to adopt a child,and teach him how to knit,
    and call him Adolf Diggler.
I'm so postmodern that I breakdance in waiting rooms, play Yahtzee in
    nightclubs, at three in the afternoon.
I'm so postmodern I only go on dates that last thirteen minutes, via walky
    talky, while hiding under the bed.
I'm so postmodern I invite strangers to my house, and put on a slide show
    of other people's nans.
I'm so postmodern I went home and typed up everything you said, and
    printed it out in wingdings, and gave it back to you.
I'm so postmodern I held an art exhibition – a Chupa Chup stuck to a
    swimming cap, and no one was invited.
I'm so postmodern I make alphabet soup, and dye it purple, and pour it on
    the lawn.
I'm so postmodern I request Hey Mona on karaoke, then sing my life story
    to the tune of My Sharona.
I'm so postmodern I write four thousand-word essays on the cultural
    significance of party pies.
I'm so postmodern I recite Shakespeare at KFC drive thru's, through a
    megaphone, in sign language.
I'm so postmodern I'm going to watch the Olympics on a black and white
    TV, with the sound down.
I'm so postmodern I go to the gym after hours, push up against the door,
    then cry myself to sleep.
I'm so postmodern I wrote a trilogy of novels
    from the perspective of a possum that Jesus patted once.

DiSCUSSiON

C. The 'Bedroom Philosopher's' take on postmodern belief and behaviour provides a humorous and satirical lampooning of postmodernism.

What aspects of the postmodernism milieu do you see reflected in these song lyrics?

PeRCEPTiON

1. What appear to you to be the most appealing aspects of postmodernism as a way of viewing the world?

2. What are its most identifiable weaknesses?

INTERVIEW
emma wright

When Emma Wright talks of her love for movies, going into the city to dance or have dinner with her friends she sounds like any 21-year old. The same is true when she speaks of her fondness for more solitary pursuits—playing the piano, listening to hip-hop and writing stories. What makes her more unique is her passion for studying philosophy, which, she admits, is not only the focus of her university degree but something she reads 'in my own time'.

Emma is in familiar territory responding to questions on worldview. Her intelligent and precise answers reveal a strong Christian faith born out of much wrestling and questioning; a quest for the truth that Emma suspects will be a life-long pursuit. Her goal to be a Christian philosopher comes down to her desire to 'share what I believe to be the truth about God with people', she says. She offers no robotic answers, but independent thought that defies any Christian stereotype or parody.

When Emma considers the big challenges facing young people today she senses a general search for purpose. 'There is a deep desire in everyone to be able to look back on their life and say it was worth it and that it meant something', she says. 'The dominant message of the culture regarding satisfaction is 'follow your heart's desire, do what you want, whenever you want and you'll be happiest if you do, without reference to any external source of advice or wisdom,' suggests Emma.

Emma senses a general cynicism among people of her generation that she describes as 'a distrust of any ideology or any practice or any kind of religion, or any kind of hope that purports to be overarching.

Chances are, if something [sounds] too good to be true, then it probably is', she says, summing up the attitudes of her peers.

When Emma speaks of the great hope that her faith brings her, there is not a hint of naïve, idealistic notions of an easy life, that some might imagine a life of faith to be about. Christian or not, she understands the world to be a 'dangerous' place and the potential for suffering in any life to be very real.

Her optimism emerges out of her sense of what it truly means to be human; an identity Emma says, that comes from God. 'I believe that one can be more or less fully human according to how well you are prepared to live out God's will', she says.

The great hope in Christianity for Emma lies in the promise of life in the new creation beyond this world. Meanwhile, she says her trust in Jesus provides deep satisfaction and peace she believes can come only from the author of life itself. 'From what I can see of all the worldviews that are on offer ... Christianity promises ... the best fulfilment for the desires and needs that we have.'

Turning her thoughts to questions of right and wrong, Emma has little time for an overly subjective view. 'I think a lot of people pretend that there is no objective right and wrong, but I think it is impossible to have no convictions whatsoever about that ... I think no matter what we say ... there are certain things that repulse us morally and certain things we delight in'. she says.

Embedded in an academic field that she admits is often openly antagonistic to Christianity, Emma has spent considerable time thinking about why it is that people are resistant to the faith that she follows. 'I think a lot about the suffering in the world and so I can really understand the point of view of some non-Christians that there just doesn't seem to be any overarching purpose to all this and therefore "how can there be such a thing as God?"—I do feel the weight of that sometimes.' Yet for Emma, the belief that somehow God is in control remains strong.

As Emma observes her friends who are not Christian believers, she maintains that for many of them, despite appearances to the contrary, spiritual questions are never far from their minds. 'When in the face of [for example] a natural disaster and when lives have been lost and we ask, "why did that happen?", I think we are asking for a religious explanation because there is no point in asking the question 'why?' if there is no 'one' that you are addressing it to—if the universe is dead then your 'why' is kind of meaningless,' she says.

Meanwhile, Emma's journey of faith continues to offer her challenges, direction and purpose. She senses in herself a less simplistic perspective on life than she once had, but one that is no less convinced of the beliefs of her childhood. 'There are a lot of questions still to be answered', she says, 'and that is what I hope to use my philosophy for'.

UTILITARIANISM

CHAPTER 4

Whatever it takes

UTILITARIANISM

Andrew Cameron

INTRODUCTION

SCENARIO ONE

You are hiking through a South American jungle, and you look forward to cooling off in a nearby village. But as you emerge from the jungle you see twenty Indians lined up in the village square. Pedro, a revolutionary, is ranting and waving his pistol while his mercenaries stand around nursing AK47s. You are spotted and dragged over to Pedro, who explains that he was about to kill this random twenty to show that the revolution cannot be stopped. But he will greet your timely arrival with a special act of mercy. If you kill just one of the Indians, the other nineteen will go free.

SCENARIO TWO

You have just completed your PhD in chemistry. It is the only thing you're any good at, and jobs are scarce. You're married and a baby is on the way, your savings are running out, and your families can't really help. An older friend calls to tell you about a job. 'What is it?' you ask. It turns out that you will be a researcher in a chemical and biological weapons factory. Your friend doesn't like the place much, but he does have influence with the management. He admits that part of the reason he wants you there is because you might help limit what they do. Someone else who will advance this work greatly is very likely to get the job if you don't apply.

What will you do?

It always seems a bit unfair, when trying to think about right and wrong, to start with outrageous scenarios like these. After all, life is not usually like this. Life is mostly humdrum, and even when it's not, we can usually work out how to avoid such dilemmas (like having other job skills, or not backpacking somewhere during a revolution). These scenarios are designed to hassle those who live in a way that seems pretty decent at first. This way of living is called 'utilitarianism', a long word to express the idea: **'I'll do whatever it takes to make more happiness in the world.'** In a discussion between two famous philosophers about this idea, those scenarios were invented by the guy who is against it.[2]

Actions are right in proportion as they tend to promote happiness, wrong as they tend to produce the reverse of happiness.

JOHN STUART MILL
UTILITARIANISM,
1863

CENTRAL BELIEFS

People who live as utilitarians have several thoughts guiding them.

1. They want to be thoughtful about the future. They don't want to act first and think later.

2. They want to leave the world, or their patch of it, a little better than the way they found it.

3. Their measure for 'a better world' is whether everyone is happier or not. Even though 'happier' can be hard to pin down, utilitarians think hard about the different things that make people happy. (It is called 'utilitarianism' because it is about maximising 'utility'—an old and odd word for 'usefulness', or 'desirability', or 'people's satisfied preferences'. I'll generally stick with 'happiness' here.)

4. They want right and wrong to be a bit simpler. They don't want to get bogged down in lists of rules. Even the Ten Commandments should only be followed if they increase happiness, and when they don't, they shouldn't be followed.

5. They don't want to have too much discussion about whether some preferences are better than others (such as opera vs. mud-wrestling, or homosexuality vs. heterosexuality). A better world will simply maximise more preferences for more people.

6. They will consider their own happiness, but other peoples' happiness counts greatly. They say they are willing to sacrifice their own happiness if they have to.

7. Some utilitarians do not even limit their thinking to human 'people'. For them, any sentient being is a 'person', and they seek for a happier world where the satisfied preferences of humans and animals are maximised.

Of course, it is easy to find people who call themselves 'utilitarian', but who are actually just selfish. They do whatever it takes to make *themselves* happy. They are 'egoists': the only person who matters is their precious self. True utilitarians do actually care about others. What the egoist and the utilitarian share, though, is that they are both *consequentialists*. They decide whether their actions are right or wrong *solely* by the results of each action.

So the utilitarian *only* asks, 'will what I am going to do make more happiness in the world?' (while the egoist simply asks whether it will work for him or herself). In the examples above,

- a utilitarian hiker in South America might say, 'to kill just one, and quickly, will make just a few grief-stricken people, plus one dead person whose happiness is reduced to zero, plus some torment for me. Compare this to nineteen people who are glad to be alive, and their families and friends, and it becomes right to pull the trigger'.

- a utilitarian chemist might say, 'it's right to take this job. Someone else might take it and work hard at it, but perhaps I can go slow or do a little sabotage or influence the management. Therefore I will possibly reduce some suffering in the world; my pay cheque will also make my family and me happier; so on balance this messed-up world will be slightly better if I do that job'.

There are lots of kinds of utilitarian, each of whom has a different way to describe happiness and a different way of calculating what will make more of it.[3] Therefore not all utilitarians would give those answers. However, they all share one thing in common: that no action is just right or wrong in itself. It is not *always* right to keep a promise, or to tell the truth, or not to steal. There is nothing *intrinsically* wrong with making and using a bioweapon. There is nothing *intrinsically* wrong with killing a stranger. The test is in whether there will be more or less happiness as a result.

Of course, there's not much happiness for the people being killed, which is why it would *normally* be very wrong to kill the stranger or use bioweapons. The reduction of their happiness to zero, and the suffering of the people who love them, is what usually makes murder wrong. But in the same debate between the two philosophers, this example also appears:

- It is 1938 and you are backpacking through Bavaria, Germany, somewhere near Berchtesgaden. (The famous 'Eagle's Nest' retreat is nearby, although you know nothing about the retreat or its important owner.) Passing a stream you notice a middle-aged man thrashing and gasping for help. You dive in and drag him to safety. As he thanks you profusely, you notice his odd little black moustache. Only after war breaks out do you realise that you have saved Adolf Hitler.

Did you do the right thing? The utilitarian philosopher who posed this example thinks it very obvious that you did the *wrong* thing—although of course he will still praise you for it, since usually, saving people makes the world a better place.[4] But perhaps you can see how utilitarians measure right and wrong by *effects*, not by the actions themselves, and not by using any rules. (Some utilitarians do have a place for rules but I'll leave them out of it.)

Utilitarianism is a television scriptwriter's dream. In the police drama *The Shield*, lead detective Vic Mackey (played by Michael Chiklis) kills his colleague, who threatens to expose Vic's corruption; but Vic believes his 'corruption' is for a greater good—to minimise suffering through his own particular style of policing. In *24* Season Two, Jack Bauer (Kiefer Sutherland) threatens a terrorist's family with death, forcing the terrorist to reveal the whereabouts of a nuclear bomb.

Perhaps you begin to glimpse some of the features of utilitarianism. **Reality** is pretty much 'what you see is what you get'. Utilitarians just observe what seems to make people happy, and are not very interested in going much 'deeper'. They dislike 'metaphysics'—the various theories about invisible forces that structure our world. **Human beings**, then, are primarily a bunch of desires that need meeting. (For some utilitarians, even a *Matrix-*

Universal happiness keeps the wheels steadily turning; truth and beauty can't.

ALDOUS HUXLEY

type world where everyone is plugged in and kept artificially happy is a serious option.) What happens at our **death** is not really a relevant consideration: since we cannot see or measure that. Utilitarians would not attempt to include any afterlife happiness or unhappiness in their calculations. In all this, utilitarians are strongly 'empiricist': they think that knowledge mainly comes through observation, not through grand theories or divine revelation. Hence **right and wrong** can only be determined by seeing what works in people's lives, and by matching our actions to increase whatever works.

HISTORY

There are examples of utilitarian thinking among the ancient Greeks, but it is more interesting to notice the modern history of this style of thinking.[5] (By 'modern' I mean the last few-hundred years.) It began to take off in mid-eighteenth century England and Scotland. Scottish philosopher Frances Hutcheson's idea of *impartial* maximisation, where society should aim to improve conditions for every member, was brand-new in these class-based societies. It wasn't long before 'happiness' caught on as the criteria by which to decide what was worth maximising.

Interestingly, one of the first serious utilitarians was a well-known Christian, **William Paley** (writing in 1785).[6] He loved the way God had made the world for our enjoyment. It followed that God's rules must be for our happiness, and that any rule worth having, and any act worth doing, must be explicable in terms of whether it contributes to our enjoyment of life. He also thought that only some things truly made people happy: relationships, passionate engagement in tasks that matter, good habits, and good health. Everything else that has the *appearance* of bringing happiness (such as sensual pleasure, the absence of pain, or greatness of rank) was actually a fake. He also thought that our prospect of happiness (or

Utilitarianism is a way of facing moral issues without God.

GENE EDWARD VEITH, JNR.

not) after we die was relevant to calculating the rightness of actions.

Jeremy Bentham wrote in response to Paley in 1789, beginning with these famous sentences. 'Nature has placed mankind under the governance of two sovereign masters, *pain* and *pleasure*. It is for them alone to point out what we ought to do, as well as to determine what we shall do.'[7] Here was the first major change to Paley's approach: that there was no point listing the kinds of happiness that were 'fake' versus 'real' (and he would later write that it just doesn't matter if one enjoys poetry or the simple game of push-pin).[8]

Secondly, Bentham thought that since we are not able to measure happiness (or unhappiness) after we die, it is irrelevant in calculating what is right. Thirdly, you will notice that for Bentham humanity finds guidance in 'nature', not in God.

Bentham laid the foundations for utilitarianism as we know it: right behaviour consists in doing *whatever it takes* to increase happiness—*of all forms*; impartially—*across all members* of a society; and secularly—*without reference* to God.

The next major utilitarian, **John Stuart Mill**, wrote in 1859 that Bentham had given civil law a whole new basis. For Mill, English law had been based on feudalism: 'a tribe of rude soldiers, holding a conquered people in subjection, and dividing its spoils among themselves. Advancing civilisation had, however, converted this armed encampment of barbarous warriors... into an industrious, commercial, rich, and free people.'[9] Here we glimpse what the utilitarians thought they were doing. They wanted a system of ethics that secured social order and harmony and which was understandable for merchants and other key players in an emerging new commercial order. Utilitarianism is a perfect ethic for a capitalist and consumerist society. Instead of asking 'is it right?' people can simply ask 'will it work?' and make a calculation, sometimes quickly, about whether the world will be better as a result.

Australian philosopher **Peter Singer** is a high-profile contemporary utilitarian. His *preference utilitarianism* consists in the maximisation of preferences or choices for the greatest number of all rational, choosing persons (including higher animals), and in the minimisation of pain for all conscious life forms. All acts and policies should achieve these ends. Among Singer's conclusions are:[10]

- Contraception, abortion and infanticide are permitted on the basis that it is always good to reduce overpopulation. (But we should not inflict pain upon sentient beings, or limit choice making for rational persons; therefore we must not kill just anyone to reduce overpopulation.)

- Animals should not suffer for something so frivolous as cosmetic testing.

- We should kill sentient beings who are painfully, terminally ill with no prospect of recovery (euthanasia), because their suffering outweighs any pleasure that life might give them.

- Actions causing pain or destruction of sentient beings (whales, for example) are wrong, but similar actions upon non-sentient beings (new-born anencephalic [no-brain] humans, or human embryos) are not wrong.

- The killing of disabled babies is justified in view of their likely suffering outweighing whatever preferences they might be likely to fulfil.

The appeal of preference utilitarianism lies in (i) its appearance of scientific objectivity; (ii) its supposed simplicity for measuring the good of social policies; (iii) the way it highlights our responsibility for the consequences of our actions; (iv) its promise to arbitrate across pluralism, and without recourse to religion, for an ethic agreeable to all; and (v) its straightforward practicality—it produces great sound-bites.[11] This kind of utilitarianism is the dominant ethic guiding law making in the modern West, and especially in Australia (although there is enough 'human rights' thinking in the mix to mean that we are not purely utilitarian).

SINGER LOGIC

Peter Singer is controversial and extreme in his articulation of a Utilitarian vision for life. His directness becomes helpful in understanding the implications of this mode of thinking. Its basis is easily identified:

> 'When we reject belief in God we must give up the idea that life on this planet has some preordained meaning', he writes. 'Life as a whole has no meaning. Life began, as the best available theories tell us, in a chance combination of gases; it then evolved through random mutation and natural selection. All this just happened; it did not happen to any overall purpose. Now that it has resulted in the existence of beings who prefer some states of affairs to others, however, it may be possible for particular lives to be meaningful. In this sense some atheists can find meaning in life.'[12]

Meaning comes from what Singer refers to as a preferred state of being. It is all about maximising happiness, which sounds fine but carries some alarming implications. Moving far from the notion of the sacredness of human life, Singer believes if a baby is disabled it makes perfect sense to replace it with one who is not, thus increasing the chances of overall happiness. He writes, 'when the death of the disabled infant will lead to the birth of another infant with better prospects of a happy life, the total amount of happiness will be greater if the disabled infant is killed'.

Much of this stems from Singer's understanding of personhood coming from consciousness, rather than a human nature or membership of the human species. To him it makes perfect sense to make judgments of the worthiness of human life according to his utilitarian framework. This is a far cry from a Christian understanding of each life being 'inviolable, unrepeatable, and irreplaceable'.[13]

IMPACT

Westerners, then, are deeply utilitarian in their outlook, exceptionally so compared to many other people in the world. Indeed if you are reading this as a Westerner, you may have been thinking 'so what? Isn't utilitarianism obvious?'

But a close examination of utilitarianism reveals some of its shortcomings. It is too simplistic, and does not make sense of everything. Utilitarianism doesn't help us with some good things that we want to protect. We will have more to say about some of those failures in what follows.

A NECESSARY EVIL? ATOMIC UTILITARIANISM

On 6 August 1945 the US airforce B-29 bomber, the Enola Gay, took off from an airbase on the island of Tinian in the West Pacific headed for the Japanese city of Hiroshima. On board was 'little boy', a bomb containing 60kg of uranium. At 8.15 the bomb was dropped over the target. It exploded about 600 metres above the city and instantly killed around 70,000 people. The death toll from this attack is estimated to be over 100,000, many died from radiation poisoning. This action on behalf of the US government was repeated three days later, when the city of Nagasaki felt the fury of the nuclear bomb code named 'fat man'. Again the death toll was horrific – reaching around 80,000 people. As in the case of Hiroshima, almost all those killed were civilians.

The decision to use nuclear weapons to bomb Japan is a striking example of utilitarian thinking. It also encapsulates something of the complexity of making moral judgments and ethical decisions by way of a utilitarian mindset. The destruction of Hiroshima and Nagasaki has been defended on the grounds of an attempt to minimise the loss of life that would have resulted from an invasion of Japan. The Japanese appeared determined to fight to the bitter end, even when defeat was inevitable.

The bombs were used to demonstrate the futility of dragging the war on, and to save the lives of allied soldiers, as well as avoiding more Japanese deaths. An end to the war was certainly achieved.

A costly invasion of Japan was avoided. Yet questions linger over the wisdom and morality of the decision. The disastrous impact on innocent civilians is inestimable. Not to mention the dark shadow the threat of nuclear war has cast over all our lives ever since.

In a speech given at Oxford University in 1956, Elizabeth Anscombe protested the awarding of an honorary degree to President Truman, 'the man who pressed the button', of the bomb. Her main argument was that to kill innocent people as a means to an end is always murder.[14] She didn't get much support on the day, yet, she highlights an interesting aspect of the debate. Was the utilitarian approach right, or did the cost of the action outweigh the benefits?

CONTACT AND DEPARTURE FROM CHRISTIANITY

It is worth pausing to notice something obvious about utilitarianism that is easily missed. Bentham may have stripped God out of Paley's utilitarianism, but he retained two important elements: (i) that it is good for every human to be considered impartially; and (ii) the way 'nature' reveals that it is good for humanity to be happy. These claims are utilitarian bedrock. Almost everyone in modern western nations would agree. They seem obvious to everyone, and do not seem to need any religious belief to make them true.

'What should we do collectively?' is the much more the characteristically utilitarian question than is 'How should I live personally?'[15]

ROBERT E. GOODIN

But—how do we *know* these claims are true? In fact, we do not. It could just as easily be the case that humanity evolved for no reason, and has no purpose, and will die painfully and pointlessly. It could just as easily be true that the strong should rule over the weak and do what they want with them. 'Nature' could just as easily be read in this way, and many social systems have proceeded on that basis. From the ancient world one need only think of the Roman Empire and its belief, implemented with brutal efficiency, that 'might equals right'. In the

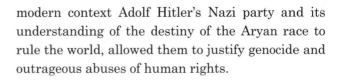

modern context Adolf Hitler's Nazi party and its understanding of the destiny of the Aryan race to rule the world, allowed them to justify genocide and outrageous abuses of human rights.

In contrast, English utilitarianism grew out of English Christianity. Eighteenth century Englishmen thought and wrote as if they agreed with Christianity's claim that God's creation was good and enjoyable, and that every person was a precious creature made in God's image. Mill claimed that 'civilisation' had produced 'an industrious, commercial, rich, and free people'; but what exactly is 'civilisation'? Certainly Christianity was a potent force in making English society 'civil' in this way.

Secular thinkers today generally have little interest in this observation, and think that we can assume the ethical results to be true even if the Christian origins are now obsolete. But Christians disagree. They would argue that without God's good news that his creation is good and that humans are precious to him, human societies *will* drift back into powerful and abusive hierarchies like the ancient ones.

Many objections to utilitarianism have been raised.[16] Here are a few, which can also be shown to have Christian roots.

1. **Utilitarianism can be unjust.**
   Utilitarians don't really want to be like this, yet they often find themselves musing over whether Jack Bauer, or Detective Vic Mackay, or Pedro's unwilling triggerman, were right. When killing one innocent person would save the lives of many, they must usually answer that the killing would be right. It is often quite hard for a utilitarian to uphold 'human rights' or 'justice' (although 'preference utilitarianism' tries hard to avoid this difficulty).

2. **Utilitarianism can be irresponsible.**
   Since utilitarians focus upon the future, the

goodness or badness of the here and now, and of previous utilitarian future-calculations, can go un-assessed. 'Don't cry over spilt milk', the utilitarian has to say. 'There's no point blaming anyone; let's just make the best of a bad job.' In this way utilitarians never have to pause and consider if their last utilitarian experiment was a failure, or if their theory is flawed.

3. **Utilitarianism can miscalculate.**

Perhaps humans are just not very good at calculating the future. Our imagination fails to notice bad outcomes all the time. Short-term consequences can't be predicted with certainty and long-term consequences can't be predicted at all. Perhaps calculating happiness is not easy, either. Peter Singer thinks the severely disabled suffer so much that it is justified to kill them at birth. But many disabled people disagree, and report they are glad to be alive despite their difficulties. In their case, Singer's calculation about them would simply have been wrong.

4. **Utilitarianism can become shortsighted.**

Leaders can descend into giving a nation what it wants (e.g. lower taxes), and not what it needs (e.g. sustainable energy sources). Governments that are focused upon people's wants leave no place for a leader to suggest that those wants are misguided. Such a society will aim for economic growth at all costs, with few asking if difficult issues are being ignored (such as an over-reliance upon fossil-fuels, or growing unease about having and raising children).

5. **Utilitarians can lose their 'integrity'.**

If a utilitarian is to be consistent, he or she can't always be honest. A utilitarian living among devout religious believers might decide that the greatest good is advanced by using religious arguments to get the best result. The utilitarian doesn't really believe those arguments, yet uses them as if she or he does. Also, the utilitarian who cares for rare flowers, or art, or heritage buildings might have to put aside this concern if these preferences are better maximised by some other means. Either way, if you think that 'integrity' is important—where our concerns agree with our actions—then that integrity will corrode.

6. Utilitarians can be self-deceiving.

Utilitarian thinking all too easily slides into personal egoistic consequentialism. Not only can we stop thinking about the many and start thinking only of ourselves, we can also fail to notice the way our desires interfere with our calculations. For constantly calculating future happiness usually means we never get there: we're always onto the next calculation—which is not so different from what the Bible calls 'greed' or a lack of 'contentment'. We get tangled up in our desires: most business fraud, for example, is committed by people who have the desire, the opportunity, and a way of convincing themselves that what they are doing is not theft. The desire for money has distorted the calculation, yet the fraudulent person still thinks he or she is doing something very 'reasonable'.

7. Consequentialism destroys trust.

Although 'utilitarianism' tries to make a safe society for all, its consequentialist underpinnings are bad news for relationships. Consequentialism, you'll remember, is where an action is *only* right because of its results; therefore if lying, or promise breaking, or betrayal, or neglect gets me a better result then I'll do those things. But good relationships seem to need truth, faithfulness, loyalty, and effort, and our work and play and friendships rely on trust that grows from these things. Consequentialism makes fractured, difficult and unsafe societies.

8. **Consequentialism can be cruel and empty.**
   True story: a woman was in great difficulty in her marriage. Obviously very sad, she walked around her workplace asking people what she should do. They told her, 'whatever it takes to be happy, honey'. But she needed to know where happiness comes from. Freedom from her husband might give it, but there would also be loneliness, pain and anger. Perhaps the pain of confrontation, forgiveness and repentance might help – but her co-workers were never going to explore that, because 'happiness' was their only cure-all. Indeed their advice was probably a code for 'get out of the relationship', and a lazy refusal to consider the woman's alternatives.

I haven't argued where the above objections might be found in the Bible; but consequentialism is always an evil there. When Caiaphas says of Jesus that 'it is better for you that one man die for the people than that the whole nation perish' (John 11: 49–50), we are witnessing a pure travesty of justice —even though ironically, Jesus' death *does* save his people from being destroyed by God's wrath.

But biblical authors were interested in the future. Every ethical decision has to have an eye on the future to a certain extent, but there are clear limits and consequentialism is rejected outright. These limits include such things as:

- Christian fellowships (that is, churches, which Paul calls 'God's temple') must not be damaged (1 Corinthians 3:16–17)

- certain lifestyles are always wrong (1 Corinthians 6:9–10, 18)

- sneaky methods of evangelism are unacceptable (2 Corinthians 4:2, 6:3)

- worship of false gods is never an option (1 Corinthians 10:14; 2 Corinthians 6:16)

- truth must never be violated (2 Corinthians 13:8)

These limits are based upon what God has revealed to humanity about ourselves. We are made not only for happiness, but also for faithful and loving relationships, firstly with God and then with each other. These relationships bring responsibilities that can be expressed as rules, which we don't always like, because so often we just want to fulfil our own desires. Our desires each have a proper place, but God trains his people when to say 'yes' and 'no' to them. All this means that we can grow into people who have various patterns of action and feeling, such as those Galatians 5:22 describes as 'the fruit of the spirit', 'love, joy, peace, patience, kindness, goodness, faithfulness, gentleness and self-control'.

There *is* a problem when a good goal justifies questionable actions in working towards it. Christians are not immune to consequentialist mistakes. But they should know that consequentialism is often just what the Bible calls 'temptation', and that saying 'no' to it *drives them to imagine **truly new and alternative** courses of action that make for a better future, *and* keep trust and sanity along the way.

The Christian chemist, refusing the bioweapons job, might be motivated to find a group of sympathisers to support her and her baby while she uses her skill to write and lobby against the bioweapons industry. The Christian hiker, knowing that he cannot shoot the Indian, will remonstrate with Pedro so passionately that Pedro may be swayed. The Christian will know that Pedro is lying when he says 'you give me no alternative', and that only Pedro will be accountable to God for whomever Pedro kills. The Christian will also know that if a group of SAS commandos were to appear, it would be justice, not consequentialism, that made it permissible for them to stop Pedro. And if no commandos showed up, the Christian hiker might even have the capacity, a bit like many martyrs before him, to turn the gun on himself, if that's what it took to stop Pedro. The revolution would probably be forgotten—and guess what would be remembered in its place?

RESPONSE — QUeSTiON

1. What would be a good slogan to sum up the underlying beliefs of utilitarianism?

2. Of the eight objections to utilitarianism (pages 96-98), which do you find the most compelling?

DiSCUSSiON

A. What are some manifestations of utilitarian thinking that you have seen?

B. On what issues is utilitarianism the most attractive option?

C. How much do you agree that 'there is a problem when a good goal justifies questionable actions' (page 100)?

CLONING FOR EMBRYONIC STEM CELL RESEARCH

Much controversy surrounds a form of embryonic research called 'therapeutic cloning'. It is legal in Britain. Some parts of Europe such as Germany have banned it, but in December 2006 the Australian Government lifted its ban on the practice.

Until recently, embryonic 'stem cells' have been farmed from discarded embryos created in IVF clinics (also a controversial practice). Therapeutic cloning offers a different method for the production of embryonic stem cells. An embryo is created from an unfertilised egg by removing the nucleus of that egg and replacing it with the nucleus from another adult cell. The embryo is grown for a few days, and then destroyed either in the course of further research into clones or into embryonic stem cells, or simply because the law requires that it not be allowed to develop beyond a few days.

Some scientists believe these practices may eventually alleviate the impact or even produce a cure for such things as spinal damage and degenerative diseases, although research at this stage is so early that no long-term benefit is guaranteed.

The controversy centres on the ethical issue of when a life begins, the nature of being human and whether there is a right to life at conception.

Those in favour of the practice see no issue with it considering the potential benefits. Bob Turner, who is the father of a man made quadriplegic in an accident, strongly adheres to the 'benefit outweighs the cost' argument. On a television discussion panel he made his thoughts clear:

'My point of view on the ethics is that it's unethical not to continue [the research]. One man's ethics is another man's poison.'

Catholic priest and bioethicist John Fleming is opposed to the technique and on the same program, said this:

'An embryonic human being is just that—a human being at the embryo stage of development. It's us at our earliest moment ...We now have to make a moral, political and ethical decision on whether it's ever right to kill one human being for the benefit of others.'

Politician John Anderson was similarly opposed:

'The principle of creating an embryo, a life with potential, with the express purpose of then destroying it in the belief that that might provide benefits for other human beings is something I have a big problem with.'[17].

DiSCUSSiON

D. Where in the above issue are you able to identify utilitarian thinking and action?

E. What understanding of the world would lead one person to be in favour of the process and another opposed to it?

PeRCEPTiON

1. What appear to you to be the most appealing aspects of Utilitarianism as a way of viewing the world?

2. What are its most identifiable weaknesses?

HUMANISM

CHAPTER 5

Not drowning, waving

HUMANISM

Rod Thompson

INTRODUCTION

Luna Park is just for fun.[2] We went there as kids in the 1960s and got lost in the Mirror Maze, a marvellous mix of mirrors that distorted time and space. They also distorted me. In one mirror I was short, squat and bloated, and in another pencil-thin and elongated. There were multiples of me and in other reflections I was fragmented. The mirrors contorted and confused me and, as I recall, I couldn't find my way out of the Mirror Maze.

If we want to see a true reflection of ourselves, where should we look? Humanism says the answer to all the big questions of life can be found unequivocally by humanity looking to itself.

Humanism does not merely promote a distinct *image* of humanness. It does far more than that. *It tells a*

distinct story. It constructs a world that seeks to ask fundamental questions of human existence, but at the beginning, in the middle, and at the end, looks only at humans to find the answers.

Inevitably then, the humanist story struggles to address deep issues of reality. Moreover, it does not have a happy ending—which is ironic, because the widely adopted humanist symbol is that of the Happy Human, developed in the 1960s to represent the humanist view that 'as we only have one life to live, we should try to create the conditions which enable all to be happy and satisfied'.[3] Like Luna Park, the humanist dream is that life should be full of fun.

HISTORY

In the broadest sense, humanist thought extends from the very first attempts to understand ourselves without engaging with God, gods, or some reference point greater than humanness itself. In Western nations, such thought draws heavily on the philosophy of the ancient Greeks.[4] However humanism, as that term is commonly understood, flourished most definitively, during the period of so-called cultural Renaissance or 'rebirth' in fourteenth century Europe. Of that era, historian S.E. Frost writes:

> Man dared to assert his ability to control the world, to know its innermost secrets and, by the power of his intellect, to master its ways and turn them to his desires. Of such was the Renaissance of the human spirit. It was an emphasis upon the human in the universe, and, therefore has been called 'Humanism'. … [The men of the Renaissance] attempted to study and control nature with the knowledge and understanding which they possessed, and as such were the forerunners of modern science.[5]

Humanist thought developed to maturity during the Enlightenment of the seventeenth and eighteenth centuries and on into the modern era. Philosophers such as Jeremy Bentham (1748–1832) and John Stuart Mill (1806–1873), authors including George Eliot (1819–1880) and Thomas Hardy (1840–1928), naturalist Charles Darwin (1809–1882), socialist revolutionary Karl Marx (1818–1883), and psychologist Sigmund Freud (1856–1939), may be counted among its most influential adherents.[6]

'Humanism' is a term with a variety of meanings and flavours. It points to a number of different endeavours related to human development. For our purposes, *secular humanism*, the most influential in the West, is the focus of our discussion. It is a naturalistic philosophy that developed in reaction to theistic and supernatural approaches. It is perhaps the dominant mode of thinking in our society today. From now on, when I say 'humanism', I am referring to *secular humanism*.

The story that humanism tells is mostly about human endeavour: creative, inventive, initiating human endeavour. Humanist heroes are characterised by courage, adventure, imagination, intellect, and most of all, a brave commitment to the here and now with its challenges and promises. The archetypal humanist hero is Prometheus, in Greek mythology the creator of humankind. According to Greek myth, the goddess Athene taught him architecture, astronomy, mathematics, navigation, medicine, and metallurgy, and he passed this knowledge on to humans. Zeus, chief of the gods, was angry with Prometheus for giving humans access to such power. In retaliation, Zeus withheld fire from humanity. 'Let them eat their flesh raw', he declared. However Prometheus dared to ascend Mount Olympus. He lit a torch from the sun, hid a burning piece of charcoal in a hollow stalk, slipped away with it and delivered fire to mankind.[7] Prometheus defied the gods.

The revenge of Zeus was severe.[8] Nevertheless Prometheus' heroic actions had liberated humanity. Divine restraint was cast off! Prometheus continues to be heralded as 'the courageous Greek god who gave fire to humans, lighting the way to reason, intelligence, and independence'.[9] Paul Kurtz, leading humanist author and currently chairman of the *Council for Secular Humanism* and of *Prometheus Books*, has thus written of humanity: 'We are defined as persons by the plans and projects that we initiate and fulfil in the world. The humanist saint is Prometheus, not Christ; the activist, not the passivist; the sceptic, not the believer; the creator, not the conniver.'[10]

Exactly how the human story actually began is not a primary concern of humanism. Some secular humanists are atheists; others are agnostics. However, all are committed to *naturalism*: that is, to the belief that 'the universe is all that there was, is, or ever will be; that it operates according to natural laws and natural processes; and that all reliable knowledge about it comes through the application of the scientific method, the naturalistic method that relies on logical reasoning and empirical evidence as the sole source of reliable knowledge'.[11]

House faith

The popular TV series *House* portrays a brilliant doctor, Gregory House, whose determination to solve mysterious medical cases is matched only by his disregard for the sensibilities of his patients.

An exchange between Dr House and one of his patients, a nun, is revealing. It gives voice to a naturalist framework that would fit well with humanist logic and trust in the power of human reason and technology over against religious faith.

Augustine (the nun): Why is it so difficult for you to believe in God?

House: What I have difficulty with is the whole concept of belief. Faith isn't based on logic and experience.

Augustine: I experience God on a daily basis, and the miracle of life all around. The miracle of birth, the miracle of love. He is always with me.

House: Where is the miracle in delivering a crack-addicted baby? Hmmm? And watching her mother abandon her because she needs another score. The miracle of love. You're twice as likely to be killed by the person you love than by a stranger.

Augustine: Are you trying to talk me out of my faith?

House: You can have all the faith you want in spirits and the afterlife, and heaven and hell, but when it comes to this world, don't be an idiot. 'Cause you can tell me you put your faith in God to get you through the day, but when it comes time to cross the road, I know you look both ways.

Augustine: I don't believe he is inside me and is going to save me. I believe he is inside me whether I live or die.

House: Then you might as well live. You've got a better shot betting on me than on him.[12]

If God or gods exist, then he, she, it, or they, are unimportant. Thus, Greek philosopher Protagoras (approximately 490–421 BC), an early voice in the history of humanist thought, is reported to have stated: 'About the gods I have no means of knowing either that they exist or that they do not exist or what they are like to look at; many things prevent my knowing—among others, the fact that they are never seen and the shortness of human life.'[13]

Consequently, the essence of the story is what humans do. Paul Kurtz writes:

> As I see it, creative achievement is the very heart of the human enterprise. It typifies the human species as it has evolved, particularly over the past forty to fifty thousand years: leaving the life of the hunter and the nomad, developing agriculture and rural society, inventing industry and technology, building urban societies and a world community, breaking out of the earth's gravitational field, exploring the solar system and beyond. The destiny of humankind, of all people and of each person, is that they are condemned to invent what they will be—condemned if they are fearful but blessed if they welcome the great adventure.[14]

CENTRAL BELIEFS

The abundant life is the goal. The concerns of such a life are outlined in the *Amsterdam Declaration of 2002*—a summary statement of the humanist commitment to social morality; human reason, science and technology; democracy and the protection of human rights; personal liberty and social responsibility; and artistic creativity[16]—admirable goals that Christian believers would also seek to promote.

In the same vein, during the twentieth century, the internationally recognised humanist spokesman,

Humanism is a democratic and ethical life stance, which affirms that human beings have the right and responsibility to give meaning and shape to their own lives. It stands for the building of a more humane society through an ethic based on human and other natural values in the spirit of reason and free inquiry through human capabilities. It is not theistic, and it does not accept supernatural views of reality.[15]

INTERNATIONAL
HUMANIST AND
ETHICAL UNION

British philosopher and atheist Bertrand Russell (1872–1970)[17] expressed his humanist vision in the following words: 'To care for what is noble, for what is beautiful, for what is gentle: to allow moments of insight to give wisdom at more mundane times and to see in my imagination the society that is to be created, where individuals grow freely, and where hate and greed and envy die because there is nothing to nourish them.'[18] Such sentiments can hardly be faulted.

In keeping with the stated priorities of Russell, the humanist story is necessarily preoccupied with moral issues or so-called *values*.[19] Asserting that God or gods cannot be known, that there is no expectation of life beyond the grave and no ultimate dispensing of justice, the humanist mind is focused on 'now' issues. And the most pressing 'now' issue, given devastating events of the late twentieth century such as the Vietnam War, and ongoing twenty-first century calamities including the AIDS epidemic, is the issue of how humans ought to behave in relationship with one another.

How should humans behave? What ought to be valued?[20] Schafersman, a humanist author, writes: 'Human ethics can only be the product of human thought. There is no God or Nature's God or Providence of Gaia that will give us ethics.' Rather, he continues: 'Humanist ethical systems must be based on human needs, human experience and human reason, not on the alleged needs or desires of supernatural deities.'[21]

HUMAN NATURE

At first glance humanism appears to have a very positive view of humanity. Certainly it is optimistic regarding the potential of human progress. Yet, according to the philosophy, humans are to be respected and valued because of their capacity for reason and creative imagination. It is their potential as rational beings that gives humans value.

Christian thinking on the other hand, tells us that humans are valuable because God values them. Created in his image, we humans enjoy a special place in the world as God's representatives, and God loves us, not because of any potential usefulness we might possess, but for who we are.[22] This is a more positive and more hopeful vision than the limited and contingent humanist perspective.

The humanist commitment is vividly portrayed in recent *Vodafone* advertisements featuring the 'common mayfly'.[23] As the insect emerges out of apparently untouched, pristine Nature, we are informed that the mayfly has a life expectancy of 'just one day. But is he miserable about it? Not one bit!'

The voice-over continues: 'He fills his day with the things he loves. He soars, he swoops, he savours every moment.' Then we are exhorted: 'Maybe there is a lesson in this for us longer living creatures. Just think, if we embrace life like a mayfly, what a life that would be! *Vodafone. Make the most of NOW.*'

Vodafone are telling the humanist story wrapped up in their own brand of technological, consumerist garb. *Vodafone* products are promoted as enhancing the humanist commitment to *spontaneity*—to the full life, to making the most of now! They bring with them a speedier pathway to happiness. And the happy life lived in the here and now is all there is. For with death, the humanist story for each individual ends.

Happiness. This is the ultimate humanist value. Happiness, indeed happiness 'now', is the defining purpose of the humanist lifestyle. And using traditional religious language, Paul Kurtz labels as sinners, 'the lazy ones who cannot, or do not, have the creative impulse' to work for happiness in their own lives and the lives of others.[24]

Millions (Motion Picture) 2004

Directed by Danny Boyle, the 2004 cinema hit *Millions* tells the story of two brothers who unexpectedly come upon a fortune in British pounds, and have only days to spend it before the currency changes to Euros.

The plot unfolds as the two boys adopt vastly different approaches to spending the money. Eight-year-old Damien decides the money has been sent by God and should be used to help the poor. Older and more worldly-wise ten-year-old Anthony, is much more in tune with the complexities of the modern economy. He is concerned with the high tax rate applied to sudden fortunes, interest rates and of course, the promise of personal gain should they spend the cash on themselves.

In Damien we have the innocence of childhood, untainted faith in God and the simplicity of his vision for how the money could help those in need. But Anthony, already in tune with the adult world, reflects a more cynical, hard-edged take on life with no room for the transcendent. He sees only what is in it for him.

Reviewer Jeffrey Overstreet says of the film:

'Best of all, *Millions* refuses to tell us that saving the world is a simple process of good deeds. It instead focuses on the differences between the brothers' worldviews, and how one's perspective can determine the fullness of one's life. Where Anthony's 'grown-up' disregard for spiritual realities lead directly to his materialism and anxiety, Damian's assumptions enable him to experience sincere joy as he serves others.'

Millions unashamedly speaks of the spiritual aspect to life that is often lost in our culture's focus on what we can see and touch. It resists the humanist creed of the inherent goodness of humanity, and rejection of the supernatural. It is clear from the way the story is told, that the audience are to think of the more spiritually minded Damien (he sees saints and communes with them) as much closer to being in touch with the real meaning and purpose of life than his more earthly-minded older brother.

There is no anticipation of life after death. Beliefs concerning immortality, heaven, hell, or judgment are scientifically unverifiable. And so, when death comes, it must be accepted with calm resolve. 'In the face of death the only thing that really counts is what has been the quality of life, and what has been given to or left for others.'[25] The achievements of the full, free, spontaneous life are the humanist legacy. In this way, each individual and each society forges its own destiny. 'The meaning of life is what we choose to give it. Meaning grows out of human purposes alone. Nature provides us with an infinite range of opportunities, but it is only our vision and our action that select and realise those that we desire.'[26]

And so the humanist story begins and ends with humankind. In the words of *Humanist Manifesto 11*,[27] published in 1973: 'As nontheists, we begin with humans not God, nature not deity.' Subsequently the authors write: 'We can discover no divine purpose or providence for the human species. While there is much that we do not know, humans are responsible for what we are or will become. No deity will save us; we must save ourselves.'[28] For each individual that salvation can only be understood in terms of the here and now. It does not transcend the grave. There is no eternity. And for the evolving cosmos of which we are part, salvation depends on the autonomous wisdom of each subsequent generation of happiness-seeking humans.

TWENTIETH CENTURY REALITIES—EXPOSING HUMANISM'S FATAL FLAW

At one level a scan of the events of the twentieth century might give humanists considerable confidence in their beliefs. Yes, we witnessed astonishing progress in humanity's use of science and technology. People went to the moon, international air travel became commonplace, computers revolutionised the way we live, a global economy developed, unfathomable medical advances took place, and entertainment became a way of life. Even going to the dentist is now a relatively pain-free experience!

Yet twentieth century history also brings sharply into focus humanism's greatest weaknesses and ultimately its failure. The innovative flair that has given rise to much progress has also produced unimaginable destruction through the high tech weapons of war. The threat of nuclear catastrophe casts a dark shadow over our lives, environmental degradation looms as a major threat. AIDS has devastated Africa, poverty grips two-thirds of the globe while the West wallows in excess. Terrorism, genocide and hatred punch conspicuous holes in humanist optimism. Big questions must be asked of the foundation of humanist belief and theory along with its basis for hope.

CONTACT AND DEPARTURE FROM CHRISTIANITY

Worldviews may be understood as belief systems embedded in widely held stories that claim to be, and come to function as, true accounts of reality. As explained in the introduction to the book, a worldview is 'never merely a vision *of* life. It is always a vision *for* life as well.'[30] Why should anyone believe the humanist vision *of* and *for* life? Why embrace the network of beliefs embedded in this account of humanness and reality? What makes the story credible? Is it true to reality? Is it internally coherent? Is it life enhancing? Does it open up life, in all its richness and diversity, offering a truly hope-filled vision?[31]

It is important to recognise that in an ultimate sense the story of humanism is vastly different to the vision of reality presented in the Bible, the compilation of texts in which Christian worldview beliefs are embedded. The biblical word from God is:

> An account of an initially good creation, in which humans are made in the image of God, to represent him in the world, and to understand the meaning of their lives only with reference to God and his Word as starting points external to themselves.[32]

> An account in which humans disobeyed God and were corrupted by that disobedience.[33]

> An account of a good creation distorted and damaged by human disobedience, that concludes with the vision of an entirely renewed world, an eternal home of all that is true, good, and beautiful, not the result of autonomous human achievement, rather God's gift to those who have trusted in the work of Jesus Christ.

> And finally, an account in which humans can be brought into right relationship with God, other humans, and the rest of the created order, only by God's undeserved kindness or grace received as a gift through Jesus Christ.

Why be critical of the alternative humanist story? Is it so wrong to want happiness? Can one condemn the humanist commitment to spontaneity, endeavour, creativity, and the pursuit of a good life? Certainly not. In many ways, humanism stirs one to stand up and cheer. On the surface, the story the humanists tell is full of the stuff of *abundant* life: courage, optimism, playfulness, adventure, and humour. Without thinking about it too much, the humanist vision offers the sort of joy one feels on a summer's day, playing volleyball on the beach with friends. It envisions rollercoaster thrills for the rest of life.

Plainly, secular humanists share with Christians some weighty ethical concerns: for world peace, for the environment and scarce resources, for civil liberty and tolerance of diversity, for economic development and the elimination of hunger, for international cooperation and the development of a world community that transcends the limitations of national self-interest. They both lament irresponsible drug use and sexual behaviour. Secular humanists are strongly opposed to what they see as the anti-intellectual gullibility of narrow-minded believers, and this is something that thoughtful Christians also resist.[34]

A.F. HOLMES

The *Humanist Manifesto 2000* is filled with unbridled optimism. As it commences the author affirms, 'for the first time in human history we possess the means—provided by science and technology—to ameliorate the human condition, advance happiness and freedom and enhance human life for *all* people on the planet.'[35] This is ironic given that previous humanist documents (*Humanist Manifesto II*, 1973) admitted the flaws of such optimistic statements and referred to the brutality of Nazism, the limitations of science or the use of science for evil purposes, corruption and the abuse of human rights and continued racism, poverty, injustice and hatred.[36] The writer of *Humanist Manifesto II* nonetheless asserts, 'humanism formulates courageous new images of the future and generates confidence in the ability of the human species to solve its own problems by rational means and a positive outlook.'[37] We are left to wonder on what basis such confidence rests.

Ultimately, it is not that humanism is too optimistic. It is not optimistic enough. It does not promise too much. Finally, it promises very little at all and secures nothing.

What makes such humanist confidence finally hollow? Why is this positive humanist outlook unable to address the deepest needs of the human condition?

Mainly because for all the humanist talk about ethics, there are *no foundations* within the humanist story for values. For all their ethical affirmations and moral discussions, humanists cannot answer questions such as, 'Whose morals?', 'Which ethical norms?', 'What truth?', and most urgently, 'What constitutes a truly good life?' Indeed, having declared happiness to be the ultimate meaning of human life, all other issues of truth come to be evaluated in the light of one's response to the question, 'Does it make me happy?'

For example, in his discussion of the contours of the good life, Paul Kurtz affirms, 'sin' is refusing to embrace the full range of self-seeking pleasures available to humans. In this context, sin is falling short of the mark of pansexualilty. It is being closed to sexual multiplicities.[38] Within the humanist story, faithfulness to a husband or wife, or the choice of celibacy, are portrayed as reductions or even betrayals of human freedom.

Having eliminated God from the story and elevated humankind to the heights of evolutionary status, there are no greater ethical foundations within the humanist story other than those that humans themselves make up. And in an evolving world, with new knowledge constantly gained through new science and technology, ethical norms are always up for grabs. Humanist ethics *must* be relative and situational—that is, they are necessarily always under revision. They cannot be fixed. They must remain subject to changing situations and competing views concerning right and wrong.

In the humanist story, human beings assume the responsibilities of divinity—merely an evolved divinity—nevertheless the fittest of a multitude of random species that find themselves in a world that is at best, uncaring, and at worst, hostile. And for humanists, the world itself is necessarily conceived of as cold and mute, an unfeeling Nature governed by impersonal laws without design or purpose.

The humanist story envisions no dignified origins and no eternal hopes. It offers no power to change the human heart. It hopes for no creational renewal. It expects no grace and allows for no miracles. There is no God of love and finally nothing in which to believe—apart from oneself. And so Bertrand Russell, philosophising out of the humanist story, envisioned the plight of humanity in the following terms:

> Mankind ... is like a group of shipwrecked sailors on a raft in a vast sea at night. There is darkness all around. One by one they fall off the raft into the waters and disappear. When the last man has fallen off, the sea will roll on and the holes made in the water by their bodies will be covered over. Nature cares not for man.[39]

The image is without hope. And finally, so is the humanist story.

Nevertheless, the humanist search for the good life is understandable and fundamental to human existence. In the Bible the writer of the Psalms sought to determine what it meant to love life and 'see many good days'.[40] His quest led him to the righteous God who was the source of the good life. Subsequently, Jesus Christ asserted: 'I have come that they may have life, and have it to the full',[41] promising true life to those who followed him.

In the second century, Irenaeus (130–202), bishop of Lyons, wrote, 'the glory of God is a man fully alive'.[42] In the Christian account of a created, distorted and being-redeemed reality, the vision of a full life is grounded in the gracious gift of God through the death and resurrection of Christ. The pursuit of personal satisfaction is subsumed by a deeper comprehension of genuine joy. Spontaneity is expressed through wisdom. Adventure is shaped by faith and love. Moreover, true blessing flows out of the Christian understanding of new life in Christ by the power of his Spirit—indeed, of being part of an entire new creation that will culminate in the renewal of the universe. Here is something more than the selfish pursuit of pleasure; something far greater than individual happiness.

Merely gazing at oneself, particularly through a distorted mirror, does not help in coming to grips with the most fundamental issues of human existence. Such a gaze may bring temporary relief but finally it can only mask reality and heighten human despair, reflecting a deceitful illusion of real happiness. Such is ultimately the case with the story of life as told by humanism.

RESPONSE

QUeST¿ON

1. **What would be a good slogan to sum up the underlying beliefs of humanism?**

2. **The author claims that the humanist story is not optimistic enough and does not promise enough (page 119 and following). Do you agree with him?**

My philosophy, in essence, is the concept of man as a heroic being, with his own happiness as the moral purpose of his life, with productive achievement as his noblest activity, and reason as his only absolute.[43]

AYN RAND, APPENDIX TO
ATLAS SHRUGGED

DiSCUSS¿ON

A. What appear to be the major differences between humanism and Christianity? How significant are these differences?

B. Where are the strongest points of contact between humanism and Christianity?

ATLAS SHRUGGED
AYN RAND AND OBJECTIVISM

First published in 1957, the novel *Atlas shrugged* clearly articulates Ayn Rand's philosophy, known as Objectivism. Objectivism would sit loosely under the banner of humanist thought, although it has its own particular understanding of reality that not all humanists would agree with.

Massively popular in the 1950s and 1960s, *Atlas shrugged* was 'the' book and was studied at universities across the world. The novel has had a resurgence of interest in recent years according to a report in USA today. A large survey conducted in the USA on the top books that made a difference in people's lives, voted the novel second only to the Bible in terms of its influence.[44]

The novel explores the premise of 'real life achievers,' the innovators and leaders in technology, medicine, art, the inventors, the researchers, and productive people, becoming so fed up with those who feed off their good work that they go on strike. What follows is a massive collapse of civilisation, kept alive by a few heroic individuals who usher in a return of culture.

Many business leaders speak of the novel as having a direct and shaping influence in their lives.[45] Others see it as naively optimistic and delusional when it comes to testing ideas against the reality of human nature and the imperfections of the capitalist system.

A leading character in *Atlas shrugged*, John Galt, gives voice to Rand's philosophy:

Man cannot survive except by gaining knowledge, and reason is his only means to gain it. Reason is the faculty that perceives, identifies, and integrates the material provided by his sense. The task of his senses is to give him the evidence of existence, but the task of identifying it belongs to his reason, his senses tell him only that something is, but what it is must be learned by his mind.[46]

In the name of the best within you, do not sacrifice this world to those who are its worst. In the name of the values that keep you alive, do not let your vision of man be distorted by the ugly, the cowardly, the mindless in those who have never achieved his title. Do not lose your knowledge that man's proper estate is an upright posture, an intransigent mind and a step that travels unlimited roads. Do not let your fire go out, spark by irreplaceable spark, in the hopeless swamps of the approximate, the not quite, the not-yet, the not-at-all. Do not let the hero in your soul perish, in lonely frustration for the life you deserved, but have never been able to reach. Check your road and the nature of your battle. The world you desired can be won, it exists, it is real, it is possible, it's yours.[47]

DiSCUSSiON

C. What elements of humanist philosophy can you detect in Ayn Rand's ideas and from the passages of *Atlas shrugged?*

PeRCEPTiON

1. What do you find to be the most appealing aspects of humanism as a way of viewing the world?

2. What are its most identifiable weaknesses?

NARRATIVE

mid-term break

The four-day Easter break couldn't come soon enough for Matt. He had been labouring over a big paper that had to be in before he left. The relief and anticipation of freedom he felt dropping it into the box, caused him to break into a run. He was tired but excited by the prospect of getting home and catching up with old friends.

Slinging his bag onto his bed, he looked around the room he'd grown up in. His old school books, fading posters and a pin board full of photos curling at the edges were all still there—really it was the room of a younger boy now, and Matt smiled knowing his Mum liked to keep it this way. Oh well, the old knick-knacks were kind of comforting to him also.

'Will Suzie be over this weekend?' his Mum asked hopefully, as he inhaled his favourite breakfast of pancakes, maple syrup and bacon—a family tradition left over from their years in North America. 'Nah, don't think so', Matt replied without further explanation.

It felt good to be home and to see his little sister who was less annoying these days. But despite the many questions about Uni and the courses he was doing, Matt didn't feel like talking about it. Somehow any explanation would be inadequate.

A big night was planned at the 'Arms' where heaps of the old gang would congregate for a reunion, although the truth was many of them had never left—would never leave. When Matt entered the old pub where he had first dabbled in underage escapades of false I.D.s and peer-inspired bravado, he was pumped for a big night. There were hugs, back slapping, nick-names resurrected, and cheek kisses for the girls. Old jokes and reminiscing; high-fives and loving insults.

Jack was there, back on leave from the Police Academy. Bursting out of his too-tight t-shirt, he was full of dopey smiles and whatever it was that drew girls in like moths to a flame. Mostly they were on a rescue mission. Rob hadn't left. His Dad's real estate business the only thing he was ever interested in. Georgia was looking even better than the last time Matt had seen her. She talked with machine gun speed and precision about her architecture degree. It wasn't a stretch to imagine her designing the skyscrapers of the future, dominating boardrooms and receiving awards. Matt enjoyed hearing her news, but predictably the conversation didn't ever turn to how he was going.

Ever the clown and always the loudest, Murray made a carefully timed entrance, late and already drunk. Immediately taking centre stage he blundered into his comedy routine that always drew a laugh. There was something menacing about Murray, and these days the response to his 'stand-up' performance had a forced feel to it. Matt knew Murray liked him 'cause they had played Rugby together; Murray's only real criteria for friendship, but these days Matt found him tiresome.

Ashley was home after her first term at visual arts college. They'd been good friends at school and he hadn't expected to see her. This was the best surprise of the night. She was moving forward, was more worldly, had a new tatt.

Matt was glad to see Nic, one of the quieter guys and a really good bloke. He'd begun his civil engineering course and they shared some tales of early university jitters. So far their experiences were remarkably similar. Both had branched out into areas they never thought they'd go. Nic, who barely said a word in school, had joined a drama society at the university and had a small part in a play. 'It's non-speaking', he'd laughed. Matt's eyes bulged as he talked about being roped into a debating team. 'It's just a college thing and not all that serious', he assured Nic.

As the night wore on, there were conversations that Matt dropped in and out of. He was having a good time. But increasingly he found himself sitting back and observing what was going on. He wondered whether people really are like his sociology professor described them, rats in a cage socially conditioned by their environment. Watching his friends go through the old routines, Jane and Tim fighting loudly, then making up and all over each other in an alcohol-induced melodrama, only added weight to his concerns. 'What does that make me?' he thought.

Just before midnight Murray climbed on a table to lead the song they'd adopted as their own in the last years of school, a rocking anthem they would all belt out with the gusto of a group united in common purpose, romantic dreams and naïve optimism.

Matt was sitting at a table with Rob when the music swelled into full swing. He joined in and laughed as the familiar words washed over him crucifying the original tune. If the music police were around they'd all be hauled off to prison without reasonable defence. Matt caught Ashley's eye from across the room. She wasn't singing and winked at him and smiled as she dragged on a cigarette. Mid-way through the first chorus, Matt too found himself going quiet. He sat and watched while Murray screamed above him, clinging to the past, desperation etched across his face.

Matt's phone beeped signalling an incoming message. 'Live the truth that is yours', it said —exclamation marks an unnecessary indication of a joke. It was Francesca from uni repeating something they'd heard in a tutorial and both struggled to contain their laughter at. 'What's that about?' yelled Rob over the din. 'Nothing mate, don't worry about it', said Matt. 'Hey, good to see you, I'll catch you later.' With that Matt waved to Ashley, and slipped out the back door into the night.🆂

CHAPTER 6

Freedom to choose

LIBERALISM

David Koyzis

INTRODUCTION

> There is no such thing as society.
>
> MARGARET THATCHER

Example 1: On the way to work you decide to stop by the local corner store to buy a newspaper and a stick of gum. This is something you do almost every day, rarely giving it a second thought once the purchase is made. You may or may not recognise the clerk at the till, and you certainly cannot be said to have entered into a lasting relationship with that person. You have connected only briefly in a superficial fashion, and that's it. You're out the door and on your way. Presumably the transaction is mutually beneficial, but neither of you is changed by the experience. You retain your freedom as individuals and go your separate ways. Your obligations to each other end once the purchase is made, and of course at any time you may decide to stop going to that store and change to one that has a better selection of newspapers. The 'rejected' clerk will not serve you with a summons or ostracise you if he or she sees you on the street.

Example 2: You have been invited to become a member of a local camera club. The group specialises in nature photography and its members have won awards at art shows. Because you like photography, you decide to join. You remain a member for two years. At the end of that period, because you wish to improve your physical fitness, you decide to quit the group and join an amateur football club instead. No-one raises a fuss when you leave, because both groups are voluntary, with members coming and going at their discretion. You are *free to join or quit* such an association.

What if every human relationship was like the variety store purchase? What if every community were like the camera or football club? What if we were to enter only into those relationships that obviously benefited us and that we genuinely *wanted* to enter? What would the world be like? This has been the historic dream of liberals since the beginning of the seventeenth century in England and elsewhere: to conceive of human relationships, especially communities, as fundamentally voluntary in character.

HISTORY

Although liberalism is generally said to have arisen in the seventeenth century, as secularisation swept Europe in the wake of the wars of religion, one finds traces of its beliefs in the Epicurean philosophers of the ancient Greek world. Epicurus (341–270 BC) and his disciples were adherents of what has come to be called individualism, namely, the conviction that all relationships are basically contractual, like purchasing an item or joining a football club. If every obligation can be reduced to contract, then I cannot be made to fulfil an obligation I have not freely and willingly taken on.

In the Middle Ages the *Magna Carta* ensured a mutual check between king and Parliament in England. Liberalism really emerged as a force in the seventeenth century as a reaction to the absolutist ambitions of monarchs who were consolidating their authority over previously fragmented territories. France, England, Spain and Portugal led the way in this.

In England, an increasingly assertive Parliament eventually put in place limitations to the power of the Tudor and Stuart monarchs. This was to become the origin of modern constitutional governments in Anglo-Saxon countries. In 1688 the Glorious Revolution, toppled the Stuart dynasty and ensured that, from then on, Parliament would be supreme. This was a significant shift from the time of absolute rule—the norm in England and Europe; whereby the monarch attempted to rule with unfettered control.

By the end of the seventeenth century, this parliamentary curbing of the king's power was being defended on liberal, individualist grounds. At this time, the writings of Hobbes, and then Locke became hugely influential. Thomas Hobbes (1588–1679) was arguably the first typically modern political scientist. He was an individualist to the core, and in this way might be considered the first liberal in so far as he understood political authority to be established by a contract amongst the subjects (the social contract). Nevertheless, if Hobbes was a liberal, in the end his all-powerful political system is answerable to no-one and is a potentially oppressive threat to freedom.

The philosopher John Locke (1632–1704) followed. The ideas expressed in his *Two Treatises on Civil Government* in 1690 seemed tailor-made for a new liberal order created by the ousting of the Stuarts two years earlier. Locke's ideas had a huge influence, especially on the founding of America a century later.

Although there are elements of earlier influences, including Christianity, in his thought, the big story Locke told was a marked departure from these. Whereas Christianity's narrative sees human history as one of creation, fall and redemption, the Lockean narrative runs as follows: state of nature, social contract, civil commonwealth and, if necessary, an appeal to heaven—that last phrase a veiled reference to overthrowing a government that does not serve the self-defined needs of individuals.

Other figures in liberalism's history include Thomas Jefferson (1743–1826), Immanuel Kant (1724–1804), John Stuart Mill (1806–1873), and in the twentieth century Friedrich von Hayek (1899–1992) and John Rawls (1921–2002). Following Locke, Jefferson justified the American War for Independence by appealing to the social contract. His *Declaration of Independence* borrows heavily from Locke's *Second Treatise*. For example, Locke's belief that government's chief task is to protect 'life, liberty and property' is slightly changed by Jefferson to 'life, liberty and the pursuit of happiness'.

CASE STUDY: FRIEDRICH HAYEK
(economist and political philosopher 1899–1992)

Hayek believed altruism (care for others beyond our immediate sphere of knowledge and relationships), was a hangover from primitive, tribal experience. He believed this urge must be overcome if we are, as he described it, to 'optimise our individual liberty through rational self-centred participation in the market'.[2]

In this area at least, Hayek's description presents Christianity and the (completely) free market as incompatible.

'As an example, continued obedience to the command to treat all men as neighbours would have prevented the growth of an extended order (that is, societies within markets). For those now living within (this) order, they gain from not treating one another as neighbours but by applying in their interactions the rules of the extended (market) order ... instead of the rules of solidarity and altruism.'[3]

The followers of liberalism sought, above all, to maximise individual freedom in the face of a variety of perceived oppressive forces. For the early liberals, the primary source of oppression is government. The *English Bill of Rights* of 1689 and its American counterpart of 1791 listed an array of liberties granted to subjects against the excessive power of government, such as freedom of speech, the right to petition for redress of grievances, and even a right to bear arms. However, as liberalism developed over the course of three centuries, the early liberals' preference for small government with few responsibilities was outweighed by the notion of contract, in which individual needs take priority over the size of government. This development led eventually to the expansion of the state, initially to check the economic power of corporate monopolies, then to guarantee freedom from want and finally, in the last decades of the twentieth century, to enhance individuals' ability to choose, full stop. This last stage of liberalism has seen followers questioning a variety of longstanding institutions, such as marriage and family, on the grounds that, as currently set up, they unjustly infringe individuals' ability to live their own lives.

LITIGATION MADNESS

The extreme elevation of the individual has been a function of the dominant liberal mindset. Of course elements of this have made life much better. It gives us great comfort to know we operate in a society that has mechanisms for protecting the rights of each person. Many of us enjoy the benefits of this freedom every day and take it for granted.

But can the interests of the individual be taken so far as to negatively impact communities? The modern desire to sue and make someone else pay for our misfortune or bad judgment is a function of rampant individualism (among other things). Outrageous stories of litigation in the US are well-known. The woman awarded $4 million (reduced to $1 million on appeal) for being scalded by a hot cup of coffee she bought from McDonalds; the man who successfully sued the New York subway after he threw himself in front of a train and was maimed—his claim was the train was travelling at the wrong speed; the 500,000 sick Florida smokers who are seeking about $300 billion in damages from the top five cigarette companies.

But other parts of the West appear to be following the American model. In Australia a man who got drunk in a hotel and was left brain damaged when he was run over, was awarded $278,000 after a court found in favour of him against the hotel and the driver.

Someone has to pay for these incidents, and presumably those in favour of such a litigious climate think the cost born by the community, in either higher taxes or insurance premiums (or fare increases in the case of the subway), is worth it. The individual, in these cases is supreme.

CENTRAL BELIEFS

1 Like the adherents of other ideologies, liberals believe above all that the world belongs to us and is raw material for realising our dreams, whatever they might be.

To be sure, liberalism has not created the openly totalitarian régimes produced by socialism or nationalism. Its followers have generally not attempted to use obviously cruel means to enforce their agenda on a reluctant populace. Nevertheless, liberals have sometimes earned a reputation for engaging in social engineering —of trying to reorder society to conform to their beliefs, all the while claiming that their beliefs are not subjective and disputable, but merely conclusions that all rational persons should come to.

2. Liberals believe in human autonomy, in other words, that people should, as much as possible, be able to determine, not only how they should live their lives, but the very nature of the world they inhabit.

   Again socialists, nationalists and radical democrats would agree, but liberalism is nearly unique in locating the subject of this autonomy in the individual rather than in some community. This gives liberals a special affection for personal freedom or, as their name already indicates, liberty.

3. Most liberals recognise the reality of death, but there is certainly no view of an afterlife.

   Some liberals may believe in something like life after death, but they are likely to do so under the remaining influence of nonliberal elements, for example, Christianity or Judaism. Thomas Hobbes (1588–1679) did not openly espouse atheism, but it is evident from his writings that he was a materialist, believing that all physical reality, including human beings, is but matter in motion. Accordingly he took seriously the fact that most of his fellow English believed in an afterlife with rewards and punishments. However, the possible reality of such an afterlife lay beyond the realm of empirical investigation, a new and controversial notion for the time.

> The ideological centre of modern liberalism is the autonomous individual, presumed to be able to choose the roles he will play and the commitments he will make, not on the basis of higher truths but according to the criterion of life-effectiveness as the individual judges it.
>
> **ROBERT BELLAH ET AL**[4]

4. There is a tendency among liberals, following John Locke, to believe that the human mind is a blank slate at birth, its contents taking shape only under the influence of outside agents, such as parents, teachers and political rulers.[5]

   This is generally true although not all liberals will openly embrace a specific theory of knowledge. This leads liberals to downplay the reality of a stable human nature that might come into conflict with their social and political agenda. If human beings are capable of being moulded to suit the latter, then, despite their vaunted affection for liberty, liberals are likely to try to control the various means of socialisation, especially schools. Thus, with some exceptions, liberals are supporters of mass public (state-controlled) education.

5. Liberals differ as to whether human actions can be intrinsically right or wrong.

   Hobbes believed that in the state of nature, a condition supposedly existing prior to the formation of the civil commonwealth, 'might makes right'. The state of nature is a state of perpetual warfare in which everything is permissible as long as one succeeds in getting away with it. Locke disagreed, believing in a *law* of nature binding on everyone, even in the *state* of nature. Nowadays it is axiomatic that liberals believe in rights for everyone, but embrace no collective vision of the good. Such visions are properly within the scope of sovereign individuals and ought not to be enforced by the coercive arm of the state. However, even liberals believe it is *good* for people to possess and exercise their rights, and this inevitably colours the public policies they pursue. The upshot is in practice liberals have a collective vision of the good, even as in effect they deny it.

6. Contemporary liberals claim that no-one, especially government, should be able to tell us how to live our lives.

Of course, if an individual wishes to live in accordance with the precepts of Orthodox Judaism, Sunni Islam or Roman Catholicism, he or she is at liberty to do so. However, it is entirely up to the *individual*, whose personal choice is definitive. Accordingly, consistent liberals tend to distrust ecclesiastical *institutions*, such as the Catholic Church or the Orthodox Church, which claim the authority to teach and discipline the faithful. In the most recent phase of its development, liberalism has exalted choice for the sake of choice, as we shall see below.

A PARTY CONVERSATION

JOHN: I can't believe all the government regulations in this country! I mean how is it that a politician can tell me to wear a seatbelt and make it a law? And as for riding my bike with a helmet on, what right do they have to make me do that?

GINA: Well if you are stupid enough not to wear one, I guess it's up to you.

MEGAN: It's only trying to protect you John, can't you see that?

JOHN: What, are we in Stalinist Russia or something? Protect me! The point is, it's my choice to live the way I want. That's part of living in a democracy.

MEGAN: What about all the healthcare we have to pay for you when you fall off your bike exercising your right not to wear a helmet?

JOHN: That's not the point. Anyway, I pay for that with insurance.

MEGAN: Well John, you seem to think every law that's made is an imposition, so what role do you think the government has?

JOHN: Government should provide security, education, and some healthcare. And roads and bridges need to be built. I just don't think government should be telling us how to live. Things like censorship and legislating for moral reform make me nervous. People have to make their own choices and live the way they want. As long as they're not hurting anyone else, then that's OK with me.

MEGAN: The government has to intervene sometimes, or the community will fall apart. Take censorship for example. Sure, we want freedom of speech but there have to be limits.

JOHN: Why? When you're an adult you should be able to read and watch whatever you want.

MEGAN: Well, for instance I know you are into freedom of speech, but racist talk on the radio is unacceptable to you and rightly so. The thing is John, there are some extreme things—really sick sexual violence and stuff—that I don't want out there. When certain people are exposed to that it's dangerous for the rest of us.

JOHN: When I want someone else to tell me how to live, I'll ask them.

MEGAN: OK, whatever.

IMPACT

At the beginning of a new century it is safe to say that liberalism's long-term influence has been enormous, especially in English-speaking countries. So pervasive are liberal assumptions that Alasdair MacIntyre has observed that the contemporary political debate occurs between 'conservative liberals, liberal liberals and radical liberals'.[6] In other words, even those who claim to repudiate liberalism nevertheless in large measure manage to accept some basic liberal assumptions.

Although liberalism is often contrasted with conservatism, this is not strictly correct, since it is common for professed conservatives to adhere to liberal political principles, albeit as expressed at an earlier stage in its development, especially the small government that refrains from interfering in economic activities. Australia's Liberal Party is a good example of a 'small-c' conservative party embracing an older form of liberalism in the name of holding onto a perceived good deemed threatened by, for example, socialism. Canada's Liberal Party is a centrist party, shifting at various times towards the 'left' and the 'right' as it takes the pulse of public opinion. The old British Liberal Party, now the Liberal Democratic Party, is only a minor party, yet liberal ideas are found within both the Conservative and Labour Parties.

Once again, liberalism is connected with our word *liberty*, or freedom. Liberals easily trumpet the virtues of freedom and rightly so. This is where they are at their best. Those of us living in constitutional democracies properly value freedom of speech, religion, the press, association and so forth. Liberalism had a huge impact on the foundation of Western democracy. As liberalism has progressed through the stages in its development, different political groupings have disagreed, not so much on basic philosophical issues, but on which is more faithful to the larger liberal project. In such contexts, true socialism—as opposed to the more moderate social democracy of the Australian Labor Party and the British Labour Party—has remained a minority voice.

POWER AND PARADOX

In an article for *The Australian Financial Review*, associate professor Greg Melleuish of Wollongong University writes of the tendency of modern democracies to impose greater control over their populations, all the while seeking to protect liberal values and goals. This, he suggests, is a paradox that is being repeated around the world:

'All Western democratic regimes in the twentieth century moved towards increasing their level of control, imposing uniformity and centralisation. Initially, this was done in the name of planning and the welfare state. Some of it, at least, could be justified in terms of what went by the name of national efficiency at the beginning of the twentieth century. And there is no doubt that proper national development could not have occurred in Australia without the growth of commonwealth powers.

[Former] British Prime Minister Margaret Thatcher sang the praises of Friedrich Hayek, who was the great champion of the idea that since individuals have the best knowledge of the circumstances that affect them, they, and not some distant bureaucrat, should be making the decisions regarding their lives. But Thatcher enhanced the power of the central state to combat those elements of society, such as trade unions, that she considered to be vested interests acting against the public good.

So we encounter another paradox in an age that has become increasingly committed to liberal values. A commonwealth government [in Australia] committed to liberal values is seeking to centralise more and more power in its hands in the name of liberal efficiency and economic competitiveness.'

Melleuish asks how this continuation of a centralising drive will fit with a more complex and heterogenous society where westerners are 'taking liberal ideals such as rights, individuality and the capacity to control their own destinies much more seriously.'

Greg Melleuish 'The Paradox of power in the hands of liberals', *The Australian Financial Review*[7]

CONTACT AND DEPARTURE FROM CHRISTIANITY

Testing liberal claims

Does liberalism provide a true account of the world —and especially human culture and society—as we experience it? This does not admit a simple answer. On the one hand, liberalism has properly empowered individual people by bringing their unique identity to the fore. At one time and in virtually all pre-modern cultures, individuals were embedded in very few communities and institutions, the claims of which left little room for discretionary action on their part. Everyone remained in his station, and there was little if any social mobility. Challenging such entrenched social dynamics, liberalism provided the impetus for many of the worthwhile achievements of our society.

At the start of a new century, however, the claims of individual freedom are familiar nearly to the point of becoming trite. Standing up for one's rights may once have resonated with people as a sign of personal courage when facing oppression and injustice. But these days it can begin to look like self interest to the point of absurdity; or a way of pursuing a course of action that would otherwise be contestable. For some, almost any behaviour can be pursued in the name of asserting our rights. This has created a social climate in which potentially divisive 'rights talk' threatens to replace ordinary political deliberation.[8] In addition such talk of rights is almost always divorced from associated *responsibilities*. Such a dynamic tends to produce fractured and divided communities, although liberal theory has little or nothing to offer such a problem.

Moreover, liberalism's professed individualism does not adequately account for our common experience of community. A person walking into a secondary school classroom where class is in session will see *more than just an aggregate of individuals voluntarily coming together for a shared purpose of their own choosing*. It will be immediately obvious that it is a classroom community and easily distinguished from, say, a family. Nor is the classroom a mere voluntary association. True, the students may be voluntarily enrolled in the course, but they have not determined the subject matter or how it will be taught, which are up to the teacher and, ultimately, to the school itself.

In short, liberalism as a theory cannot match up to our common experience of human society. Because liberalism undertakes to reduce human communities to voluntary contracts among individuals, it inadequately accounts for the reality that people easily distinguish one kind of community from another, even prior to theoretical analysis.

It has been said that Marxism is a Christian heresy. The same could as easily be said of liberalism, which has a similar pedigree. Both presuppose a secularisation of Christian faith in which salvation in Jesus Christ has come to be replaced by a human project for reform or even revolution. The love of freedom certainly has biblical roots. The Exodus recounts the liberation of the people of Israel from Egyptian slavery, while Ezra, Nehemiah and the second part of Isaiah tells of the return of the Jews from exile after the Persian king Cyrus permitted them to do so. In Galatians 5:1, the Apostle Paul urges his readers, 'It is for freedom that Christ has set us free. Stand firm, then, and do not let yourselves be burdened again by a yoke of slavery.' Paul further indicates, 'where the Spirit of the Lord is, there is freedom' (2 Corinthians 3:17b). Jesus said to his followers, 'then you will know the truth, and the truth will set you free' (John 8:32).

However, while the biblical authors are concerned about achieving freedom from poverty and unjust oppression by others, their primary focus is on becoming free from the power of sin and death. According to the Bible the worst form of enslavement that human beings can experience is to their own weaknesses, failings, and evil tendencies, which are the source of other forms of oppression. Christian belief is that the ultimate source of such freedom is salvation in Jesus Christ, without which people remain in their sins, and thus in slavery.

While the Bible understands freedom to be freedom *for* living the obedient life, liberalism understands freedom primarily as freedom *from* some form of external constraint. What people do with their freedom is their own business, society—and especially the state—refraining from determining what that might look like. However, what liberalism cannot guarantee is that by maximising individual freedom, society as a whole will benefit. In its earlier stages liberalism champions the free market, assuming that self-seeking individuals will produce a kind of natural order. This 'spontaneous' order, says liberalism, is something no government should interfere with, as it would get in the way of the growth of material wealth. In its latest stage, liberalism ends up favouring an increasingly large state apparatus. It does this to compensate for the negative consequences of a society where individual freedom is paramount. Evidently there is such as thing as too much freedom.

Although some liberals recognise that freedom without responsibility is not a good thing, they generally have to look outside their worldview to find this.

Often it is Christianity, with its strong sense of individual freedom balanced by personal responsibility to the larger community that will play a role here.

RESPONSE

QUeST¿ON

1. What would be a good slogan to sum up the underlying beliefs of liberalism?

2. To what degree do you think responsibilities to communities should override individual choice and freedom?

DiSCUSSION

A. What limitations do you envisage in the way liberalism locates the subject of human autonomy in the individual rather than some community?
(See point 2 of Central Beliefs on page 133)

B. What are the most obvious points of agreement between liberalism and the Christian worldview? What makes them less easily reconcilable?

C. What is the significance of the distinction between liberal and Christian notions of freedom?
(See 'Contact and departure' page 139-143)

D. Do you agree that Christianity has a role to play in helping to establish a balance between freedom and responsibility? In what areas can you see this apply?

media

Liberty and compromise?

West Wing (Television Drama)

Josh: *What do you say about a government that goes out of its way to protect even citizens that try to destroy it?*

Toby: *God bless America!*

Liberal democratic governments are committed to assisting people to enjoy a set of basic freedoms. There are legitimate questions as to how far these governments are prepared to compromise on individual freedom, in order to protect liberty as a whole.

What if, for example, a political group or party forms that is seeking totalitarian rule, or imposition of a particular religion, or a system that would entail oppressive intrusion into people's lives? For our purposes, imagine this party has real chance of success.

Should the government allow that party to continue, on the grounds of honouring the principle of freedom? Or should it ban the group on the grounds that, while they may interfere with the freedom of that particular party, it allows for the greater enjoyment of liberty overall?[10]

Consequentialists (discussed in chapter 4) would say that you only honour a set of values in so far as you are promoting them.[11] They would be comfortable banning this group, bugging phone conversations, and arresting people if they felt they were becoming a threat.

Contemporary examples might include censorship of material that could incite hatred, or refusing a visa to a person who denied the holocaust. In the 'war on terror' many governments in the West have taken action that has restricted people's freedoms, in the name of the greater good and ultimately, they say, the protection of freedom. Civil libertarians however, speak out against these restrictions, claiming that there is enormous danger in compromising the value that a democracy holds dear. The liberal stance in this instance might seek to protect the idea of individual freedom and give this priority over a perceived safer environment.

DiSCUSSiON

E. In what situations would you be happy to compromise individual freedom for the greater good. Are there issues that you think should be 'written in stone' without room for compromise or selective judgment. What are the potential problems with such an approach?

FREEDOM AT A PRICE

In an article titled 'It's time for the Liberal party to live up to its name', Richard Allsop, research fellow of the Institute of Public Affairs, and former senior adviser in the Kennett state Liberal government in Victoria, gives a clear articulation of a liberal vision for Australian States.

Urging the party to be the party of small government, he called for a consistent liberal agenda. 'There are large swathes of state government responsibilities where the Liberal Party can position itself firmly on the side of citizens who want to live their lives free of unnecessary government-imposed rules and regulations', he wrote. Allsop then proceeded to warn against the dangers of going down the path of racial vilification laws, citing Rod Liddle's take on the British experiment in this area, 'Today you can be prosecuted for insisting that homosexuality is a crime against nature and yet also prosecuted for denigrating the Koran, a book which insists that homosexuality is a crime against nature. Let the Liberal Party be the party of free speech', said Allsop.

Market-based opportunities for development were next on Allsop's agenda. Restrictive planning regulations and prohibitive costs were placed alongside 'busybody neighbours', and 'control freak local councils' as the writer called for the market to determine policy. Presumably Allsop is not facing the prospect of the view from his bedroom becoming nothing but a brick wall any time soon!

His call for the lifting of any restrictions on shop trading hours was based on what he called a defence of the rights of the consumer. We have become used to being able to shop at any time of the day or night, but some would argue such practices, if completely unrestricted, begin to impinge on the interests of employees (who also happen to be consumers), not to mention debates that call into question the benefit of non-stop shopping. Consistent with the liberal agenda however, Allsop offers the market as the ultimate judge of what is good and proper.

He turns his attention next to the need to protect the interests of gamblers. Allsop suggests poker machine players are a group who are becoming the 'most maligned in the country'. The problems of a minority are no reason to restrict the freedom of the rest.

He says 'stifling genuine community activity' (not usually the way poker machine playing is regarded) is not the place of government.

'An agenda of personal freedom', is one that voters are likely to embrace, believes Allsop, and in that he may well be right. Yet one is left wondering if freedom of this nature comes at some price.

DiSCUSSiON

F. How does the article shed light on what might be concerning about liberalism?

G. In what areas would you see liberals most needing to compromise in their push for freedom?

PeRCEPTiON

1. What appear to you to be the most appealing aspects of liberalism as a way of viewing the world?

2. What are its most identifiable weaknesses?

alice lang

Alice Lang loves a challenge. Deeply shy growing up, she threw herself into ballet, canoeing, hiking and eventually even took on debating. Her philosophy was to deliberately put herself into difficult situations, to test herself and see what she could do.

Her choice of photovoltaic engineering, studying solar and renewable energy systems, seems to fit such an approach. 'I wanted to save the world', she laughs. Shy she might be, but at 18 and still in her first year at university, Alice exudes determination and quiet confidence—qualities evident in her answers to our 'worldview questions'. Her responses reflect someone who is clearly comfortable with her take on the world. Just as clear is a worldview that is unambiguously naturalistic. Alice, while 'fascinated' with religion has no such belief herself.

So what are the biggest questions facing young people today? 'What can I do to make a difference?', 'What does everything mean?', 'Where do I fit in?', 'Do I mean anything to anyone?', says Alice. Her observations tell her that for many people satisfying answers to those questions are hard to come by. 'There are so many options and possibilities—it is difficult to pin down one version of life or pathway through it, so that makes it difficult to get a good answer to those questions', she suggests.

Nonetheless for Alice a meaningful life comes from relationships, 'knowing you are loved and respected', and feeling you have made 'a worthwhile contribution to the community', 'Because I don't have a particular standard to hold up to life—it is difficult to say why that is a more meaningful life than others, [but] hopefully it would be a life that would do more good than harm', she says.

When considering the issue of what it means to be human, Alice leans heavily on rationalistic thinking. 'I lean towards the highly evolved machines [concept] —I think we do respond biologically to things around us', she says. According to Alice's interpretation, a key aspect of the human condition relates to consciousness, complex thinking, inquisitiveness and deep need for community.

Alice thinks the nature of the universe is 'perhaps cruel, perhaps random' and that order has developed out of chaos. 'When the atoms and the dust and the debris that form the universe were thrown out across the space that we exist in, it had no particular order, but the forces that those things created on themselves produced the order that we observe', she says. Just where that order came from Alice admits, is something of a mystery. 'I'm sure if I knew I'd be a millionaire!'

For Alice the world exists without any ideal plan or order, and while there are things about her life and the world that she would like to change, the hope of something better she believes, comes entirely from what we as humans can come up with on our own. Her motivation for working towards a better existence stems from an imaginative sense of how things could be. Such hope, according to Alice only extends as far as this world. At death, 'I think we rot', she says. 'People remember us for a few years and then its pretty much all over.' Alice says her belief in the randomness of the universe and the extinguishing of life at death doesn't present her with any great existential angst.

On the important worldview question of 'how we know right and wrong', Alice firmly resists the notion of a universal standard. In her mind 'right and wrong' are a system of values that we develop as we grow up, but these are specific to our time in history and our culture—a combination of our assumptions and our individual application of those assumptions. 'It would be kind of nice to have a perfect order to the way we think about the world [but] I certainly haven't come across it,' she says.

'The least amount of damage to the greatest number of people', would effectively sum up Alice's understanding of right and wrong, although when pushed to explain the basis for such a belief being better than any other, Alice concedes we are entering murky territory.

Alice has little hesitation when asked to point out the most appealing aspect of the Christian worldview. 'I can't pretend to know a lot about the Christian worldview but a lot of people I know who are devout Christians have a wonderful sense of morality and willingness to give of themselves to others, to help others and show real compassion to others, and those things are very appealing characteristics … the Christians I see around me are excellent examples of humanity.'

And what about the least appealing aspects of Christianity? 'I hate being told what's right', says Alice. 'I like to figure things out for myself. So I don't like the idea of there being something which gives answers.' But what if those answers are being given by God himself? 'I think that were I to become religious later in life I think I would have to discover that creator for myself', she says.

FEMINISM

CHAPTER 7

Sleeping with the enemy

FEMINISM

Mary Fisher and
Michele Smart

INTRODUCTION

Life is full of opportunities and possibilities for most young people in the West today. A young woman might plan to become an engineer or farmer. She might train to become a chartered accountant or lawyer and aim to one day make partner in a firm. Her ambitions might include being a professional surfer, dentist, dancer, rock star, or high court judge. She could seek to become an airline pilot or a bus driver, an auctioneer or an architect. She might hope to be a detective, surgeon, teacher, fashion designer or Prime Minister. She might easily be a boss in charge of employees, both male and female. Any of this she might combine with a role as mother. If she is gifted and works hard enough, one or more of these dreams might become a reality and her gender should not be an issue.

It hasn't always been this way. Until quite recently the career choices and opportunities for males and females were distinct and largely separate. Once in the not-too-distant past, regardless of how talented she was, a female simply would not have had the same opportunities as her male counterparts. Her role in society was regarded as mainly in the domestic sphere of home and family, and if she worked, it would mostly be in service activities. If a woman chose a career and was successful, she almost certainly sacrificed any hopes of marriage and family.

Today, many of the choices that are open to females, and what we would consider basic rights that women enjoy, are due largely to the struggle for equality, led by women, that began over a century ago. This struggle, known as feminism, has produced change that runs deep and has been far-reaching. Indeed this has been brought about not only through legislation, but also through a revolution in society's attitude to women.

It has changed the very air we breathe. As Ariel Levy points out, the women's movement has introduced revolutionary ideas that have 'caught on so thoroughly they now seem self-evident'[1].

> Women are told from their infancy ... that ... softness of temper, outward obedience, and a scrupulous attention to a puerile kind of propriety, will obtain for them the protection of men, and should they be beautiful, everything else is needless.
>
> **MARY WOLLSTENCRAFT**[2]

HISTORY

A scan of the treatment of women throughout history is required if we are to understand or appreciate the rise of feminist thinking. It is fair to say that through the ages (and in many countries today, particularly in the third world) women have been seen as second-class citizens, the property of either their father or husband. For the most part they have been barred from public life and have had little or no access to education. (In the West, women's education only became public policy in the nineteenth century.) Women have traditionally had few rights before the law. As recently as the early nineteenth century women underwent 'civil death' upon marrying, forfeiting their rights to their husbands.

Mary Wollstonecraft is often seen as the mother of modern feminism. Inspired by the Enlightenment's emphasis on reason and the rights of the individual, she championed the cause of women. Her treatise 'A Vindication of the Rights of Women', written in 1792, was highly influential.

Wollstonecraft was deeply frustrated by the lack of education for women. These frustrations stemmed from firsthand experience; as a headmistress the girls she taught seemed totally uninterested in learning. Rather she saw them as being obsessed with their physical appearance and ideas of romantic love. Wollstonecraft declared these girls were raised to be 'gentle domestic brutes'.[3]

The late eighteenth and early nineteenth century saw growth in educational opportunities for women. However even these were limited—the focus was on giving girls the necessary skills to manage a household. A university education was generally considered unnecessary. Even at pioneering institutions such as Oberlin College, in the USA where women were enrolled as early as 1837, no classes were held on Mondays so that women could take care of the male student's clothes![5]

Industrialisation and domestic toil

From the eighteenth century and the onset of the industrial revolution, changes that began in Britain, eventually swept throughout Europe. Mechanisation replaced a society and economy based on manual labour. Things really changed for women from this time on, particularly in the domestic sphere. Before industrialisation the household was a key economic unit, where the work of men *as well as women,* was vital. Both men and

> How many women thus waste life away the prey of discontent, who might have practised as physicians, regulated a farm, managed a shop, and stood erect, supported by their own industry, instead of hanging their heads surcharged with the dew of sensibility, that consumes the beauty to which it at first gave lustre.
>
> **MARY WOLLSTENCRAFT**[4]

women worked to provide food and clothing, and the goods and services that women sold were a vital part of a town's economic life.[6]

Industrialisation brought paid work out of the home and into the office or factory, and that paid work became the domain of men. Women found themselves more isolated in a domestic sphere, which no longer needed them economically.[7] The idea of isolated women caught in a cycle of domestic drudgery and meaninglessness was something that was taken up by what is known as 'second wave' feminism in the 1960s.

The first wave

First Wave Feminism, a retroactive term used by scholars and historians, describes the political mobilisation of women that occurred in the latter half of the nineteenth century and early twentieth century leading up to World War I. This was a divergent movement. In America it included women who had fought for the abolition of slavery as well as the Women's Christian Temperance Union. In Britain suffragettes such as Emmeline and Christabel Pankhurst were arrested, jailed and took part in hunger strikes as they sought to win the vote. In Australia various groups railed against what they saw as sexual double standards in marriages where fidelity was held as the supreme virtue of women but not necessarily men. Rose Scott campaigned to raise the age of consent for girls (from 14 to 16) and Vida Goldstein highlighted the disadvantages women faced in the labour market.[9]

The central campaign of First Wave Feminism was for the vote. In Australia the battle for suffrage began later than in Britain or the US, but had earlier success. New Zealand led the way among Western nations in giving the vote to women in 1883, Australia followed suit in 1902. It was not until 1920 that the 19th Amendment was passed permitting women the vote throughout the USA.

First Wave Feminism lost much of its impetus after the vote was won. It was not until the 1960s that a new movement emerged, what is now termed the Second Wave.

Women's lib
The second wave

Second Wave feminism, also known as 'the women's liberation movement' placed issues around sex, pregnancy and childbirth as crucial to the welfare of women. These issues were seen as important as the fight for equal rights and opportunities in the workforce. 'The personal is political' became a catchcry for the movement. Second wave feminists wanted more than just to participate in the existing political system, they increasingly pushed for revolution: a radical re-write of all institutions.

Betty Friedan's 1961 book *The Feminine Mystique* (influenced by another feminist text, *The Second Sex* written by Simone de Beauvoir in 1949) provided the impetus for the new movement. A housewife and mother of two, Friedan had no idea of the storm of controversy her work would unleash.

Read today, *The Feminine Mystique* is hardly radical, but at the time it tapped into the frustrations of a generation of post-war housewives. For many women it articulated their feelings of entrapment and oppression. Having enjoyed greater freedom and work opportunities during World War II, women found themselves back in the kitchen: the 1950s ideal was of a housewife in an apron living in domestic bliss in the new suburban sprawl. But in *The Feminine Mystique* Friedan painted a different picture. She interviewed women across America and chronicled feelings of emptiness and incompleteness, describing women as prisoners in their homes. She questioned why, in choosing marriage and children, women should be forced to choose the domestic over all else. Frieden wrote the book out of her own

experience and that of her family—Friedan's mother had to leave a satisfying job as a writer when she became a wife and mother, and Friedan lost her job as a journalist when she became pregnant with her second child.

Out of the overwhelming response to her book Friedan established NOW—the National Organisation of Women. She was a key leader in the struggle for the passage of the Equal Rights Amendment in America in 1972.

The pill and the sexual revolution

If Friedan argued that women should be able to pursue interests outside the home, it was the availability of the birth control pill that proved to be revolutionary. The pill did two things, it unleashed the sexual revolution, and it expanded women's opportunities beyond motherhood. Women were now free to pursue careers by postponing childbirth—indeed they could choose to have no children if they so wanted. Women were also free to experiment sexually, without fear of an unwanted pregnancy.

'The pill, the vacuum cleaner and the washing machine changed women's lives, not feminism.'

DORIS LESSING[10]

The women's movement agitated for the right to legalised abortion and in America the Supreme Court decision in 1973 in *Roe v. Wade* was seen as a feminist victory. Feminists also highlighted the discrimination women faced in the workforce and fought for greater options in terms of maternity leave and childcare. Women's shelters were set up as feminists forced issues of rape and child sexual abuse onto national agendas.

By the 1970s activists like Friedan had been sidelined by more radical feminists. Susan Brownmiller, Germaine Greer and Kate Millett called for the complete transformation of society. These women wanted much more than a balance of traditional family roles with work. Like de Beauvoir, they saw the institution of marriage, and indeed the nuclear family as oppressive and out-of-date. What was the point of seeking equality when the whole system was flawed; when the very institutions and discourses feminists were working within were set up by men?

The Stepford Wives (Motion picture) 2004

The 1975 film version of this story (originally a novella written by Ira Levin) presented a dark science fiction tale that played on feminist concerns that men would, if given the chance, exchange their real wives for domesticated, sexualised robots whose only desire was to please their men. There was a sinister tone to the story that reflected the seriousness of the feminist struggle in that era.

Fast-forward to 2004 and the same story had a completely different feel. By the time the community of Stepford was being represented by Matthew Broderick, Nicole Kidman and Bette Midler, the narrative had been transformed into complete comedy.

The contrast in the two versions of the story may well reflect something of the way the feminist struggle has altered course over the years, and perhaps lost some of its impetus. The later version touches on familiar gender issues—domestication in the gated community of Stepford means women cooking, cleaning, and doting on their husband's every need, all the while looking serene, sexy (in a 1950s floral kind of way) and subservient. Yet the sting has been taken out of this tale and the viewer, female or male, is only ever expected to chuckle and reach for the popcorn.

If it is a signal of the way things have changed, earlier feminists must either be sitting back pleased that the battle has been waged and won, or else wondering where it all went wrong.

movies

A splintered movement

Over time the women's movement became more divided, for example, the contentious issue of pornography created two distinct factions in response. Susan Brownmiller, Gloria Steinmen and others in America formed a group named Women Against Pornography. ('Pornography is the theory, rape is the practice' was one of their slogans.) Others, who used the term 'sex-positive feminist', saw the anti-pornographic stand as repressive and working against the sexual liberation they had fought for.[11] Any form of censorship reminded them of the bad old days before liberation. Also Friedan had a very public stoush with what she termed 'the lavender menace': lesbian feminists who were calling for more acceptance within the women's movement.

Feminism ain't about equality it's about reprieve.

ANI DIFRANCO

IMPACT

By the 1980s, fragmentation in the movement meant that feminism had lost much of its momentum. But there were other reasons the movement slowed. For one, what was once considered radical had become mainstream—university departments were now dedicated to feminist studies. Most women in the West had access to higher education, and despite the 'glass ceiling', women had moved into higher education and executive jobs, they had joined the military and they had made these choices without having to give up the idea of having children. In Australia the Sex Discrimination Act of 1984 provided legislative protection of women in the workforce against both direct and indirect discrimination.

During this time, postmodernism, psychoanalysis, and poststructuralism also had a profound effect on feminist thought, in that there was a greater emphasis on celebrating difference.

But there was also a growing gulf between feminism and the public. Naomi Wolf's 1993 book *Fire with Fire* noted dissatisfaction with feminism among women themselves. 'While a strong majority of women passionately endorse the goals of feminism, a large number avoid identifying with the movement itself', she wrote.[12] Susan Faludi's *Backlash: The Undeclared War Against Women (1991)* also suggested that there had been a reaction against feminism. She cited examples such as the strength of the anti-abortion lobby, a continuing pay gap between men and women, and declining numbers of women represented in Federal office in the US.

Where to from here?

Some commentators now claim we are living in a post-feminist world. A Sydney newspaper recently devoted its entire weekend magazine to women's issues. Tellingly, its editor admitted that it had been several years since the magazine had published a women's issue, and over that time, she said, feminism 'has become in some circles a dirty word; certainly for many, a tired word; for others, a divisive one'.[14] It seems feminism has an image problem.[15] Today with the rise of raunch culture young girls are more likely to wear their lingerie as outer-wear than 'burn their bras'. And yet, the feminist movement has indeed been revolutionary – the choices available to young women today are staggeringly different to those open even to their mothers.

Gender and equality

In any discussion of feminism issues of 'gender' and 'equality' prove contentious. Is there any difference between 'gender' (the idea of what constitutes masculine and feminine) and 'sex' (the biological differences between male and female)?[16] In the past, in the fight to win equality, many key feminists were at pains to note how similar men and women were: many saw gender-based self-understanding

It's certainly not dead, but it has broadened. One of the problems with early feminism is that it left many women feeling worthless – particularly women who were homeworkers or chose more traditional lives. But with any great movement, it takes time to find its balance.

CLARE BOWDITCH – Singer songwriter in answer to the question 'is feminism dead?'[13]

as purely a social construct within male dominated societies. The fight therefore was to free women from these perceptions and to open all areas of society to women.

Recent studies of the brain,[17] and an increasing awareness that women react to medicine in different ways from men,[18] has contributed to the debate. The diverse world of feminist theory is starting to recognise that earlier concepts claiming gender has no biological role in determining social identity are somewhat naïve. While many feminists now emphasise that men and women are indeed different, they still resist what they see as arbitrary and ungrounded distinctions between men and women, and the ensuing discrimination that comes with such distinctions.[19] This remains a worthwhile and important battle.

Raunch culture

In a recent men's magazine the lead story hails the model Elle Macpherson as a powerful woman and applauds her for her business know-how. Accompanying the article is a full photo spread of Elle in leather lingerie standing with legs apart; a fawning group of half-clad younger men lined up behind her. The overtly sexual pictures show a woman not to be messed with, a sexually empowered woman in control of her destiny.

Ariel Levy's 2005 book, *Female Chauvinist Pigs: Women and the Rise of Raunch Culture,* is a disturbing read for those with sympathies for the feminist cause. It documents our culture's growing obsession with sexuality that used to be the domain of the porn industry—Brazilian waxes and pole-dancing classes have now become mainstream. She notes the obsession with vacuous celebrities such as Paris Hilton.

Levy sees feminism's confusion over sexual liberation as contributing to the rise of raunch culture and she is deeply concerned that young girls now see the flaunting of their sexuality as a liberating 'empowering' experience.

'How is resurrecting every stereotype of female sexuality that feminism endeavoured to banish *good* for women?' she asks (her italics).

'Liberation' and 'empowerment' are still buzzwords, but they once referred to bucking the system, notes Levy. These terms have since been drained of meaning, she writes. Instead young women are conforming to a mass-produced idea of male fantasy.[20]

CENTRAL BELIEFS

Neat definitions of feminism are not easy to find. A quick scan of the various categories of feminism(s) to be found within contemporary dialogue, reveals what a complex phenomena it has become. These include: African feminism, anti-racist feminism, black feminism, Christian feminism, Hispanic or Chicana feminism, ecofeminism, libertarian feminism, Islamic feminism, lesbian feminism, male feminism, Marxist feminism, materialist feminism, nationalists' feminisms of various kinds, post-colonial feminism, post-feminism, postmodern feminism, psychoanalytic feminism, radical feminism, socialist feminism, spiritual feminism often including Wicca or witchcraft, third-world feminism, and womanism!

Because I am a woman, I must make unusual efforts to succeed. If I fail, no-one will say, 'She doesn't have what it takes.' They will say, 'Women don't have what it takes.'

CLARE BOOTHE LUCE[21]

So, like any ideology, feminism is not homogenous. Having acknowledged these variations, what can we say about feminism? Here are a few generalisations:

- Feminist movements are motivated by a concern for the welfare of women within society.

- Feminism has concerned itself with the role of male oppression of women throughout recorded history. Feminists refer to this male oppression (or male systems of privilege) as 'patriarchy'.

- Feminists have sought to eradicate oppression of women based on religion, culture, race, educational background and social class.

- Feminists are concerned about the sexual objectification of women, and violence against women.

- Feminists believe that a woman should have dominion over her own body, and thus the issue of 'reproductive rights' is a large concern for many feminists.

- Feminists around the globe strongly advocate that gender should not predetermine political and/or economic rights.

Patriarchy

In any feminist discussion, 'patriarchy' is an important term. Maxine Hancock explains the term:

> The one underlying agreement in a very often fragmented discussion is that throughout the history of humankind, there has been a consistent oppression of women by men ... The basic cause and result of this ... has been the institutionalisation within almost all societies of systems of male privilege, sometime referred to as 'patriarchy'. Patriarchy has to do with any social or cultural patterns which accord men special privilege on the basis of their maleness – when a person is born male he is born to certain privilege or position or rank which is denied a woman when she is born female. [22]

A feminist would see the following as examples of patriarchy:

- Women received the vote much later than men in most Western societies.

- Few women are in positions of leadership both in government and business.

- In the Western world women have started to gain pay equity for doing the same work as men only in the last 50 years.

- In many places in the Western world women have not had the same educational encouragement or opportunities as men until relatively recently.

CONTACT AND DEPARTURE FROM CHRISTIANITY

There is no doubt that there are many areas where feminist activities have contributed to the well-being of society from a Christian perspective. These include seeking equal educational and work opportunities for all people, equal pay for equal work, quality prenatal care for all pregnant women, seeking solutions to violence within familial partnerships, seeking to limit female circumcision or 'clitorotomies' in societies where it is practised, and efforts to combat rape and sexual harassment. These are all moves to which Christians can say a resounding 'Amen'.

When feminism has fought to oppose injustice; where it has involved a struggle against oppressive practice and violent and abusive corruption; when it has sought to provide opportunity for people to develop their gifts and have opportunity to exercise these, it has certainly been aligned with Christian thought. Indeed many committed Christians have joined in the struggle.

This should not be surprising. In the context of the Judaism of his day, Jesus was radical in his treatment of women. In a patriarchal society that largely confined women to the home, and one in which women received minimal religious instruction, Jesus treated women as equals and freely associated with them.[24] Jesus had Jewish women disciples, including Mary Magdalene, Joanna, and Susanna, who accompanied and supported him out of their private means (Luke 8:1–3). Jesus frequented the home of Mary and Martha, and ate meals with and taught women as well as men, a radical concept in the age in which he lived.

But despite Jesus' words and actions, the Christian church and feminists have had a difficult relationship. Although the Christian Scriptures give a key role to women within both the Old and New Testament, feminists have seen, in both the language and structures of the church, a patriarchy that has oppressed women.

Mary Daly, a radical feminist theologian and philosopher, not only rejects institutional religion as it exists, she perceives the church's hymns, and the male language in talking about God as a crushing tradition making women less than human; a tradition which she argues tells women that they do not exist.

For Daly and like-minded radical feminists, the foundational question is not whether the God of Christian Scripture should be called Father. Rather the radical feminists reject the very possibility of women being redeemed by a saviour who is male, that is Jesus Christ. With that rejection comes a rejection of the cross of Jesus Christ as the central event of redemption. At its foundation this sort of radical feminism is seeking independence from the God of Christian scripture. This would put it in the same category as the other systems of thought dealt with in this book, which have rejected God and set up human ideology in his place. Such a claim does not however negate the valid critique that many feminists have of contemporary culture.

Further, it would be extremely simplistic and unfair to put all feminists—female or male—in the same category as their radical counterparts. There is nothing in the struggle of moderate feminists to bolster and protect the interests of women that is necessarily counter to a Christian worldview. In many cases, it fits neatly with the Christian vision of life.

DEBATES OVER ABORTION

Most feminists see the right of a woman to have access to legalised abortion as a 'litmus test' of true loyalty to the feminist cause.[25] As such it is a legitimate means of examining the difference in worldview between some feminists and Christians.

Feminist activists have been at the front of what they call the 'debate on reproductive rights'. Others refer to it less euphemistically as the abortion debate. We need to proceed with caution here, as not all people who regard themselves as feminists are in favour of abortion.

This is an extremely complex issue, and one that understandably draws emotional responses on both sides of the debate. At the risk of oversimplifying things, we will highlight an important angle of the Christian worldview in order to explain why it is that Christians can't support termination of babies after conception.

The perspective that abortion is about the 'reproductive rights' of the individual woman arises from a broad understanding in the West of what it means to be human, that is totally contrary to a Christian worldview.[26]

In the 'reproductive rights' argument, every woman is perceived as an autonomous individual with sole responsibility to determine control of matters relating to her body and reproductive capacity. At one level this is understandable. It is not surprising that a woman in the twenty-first century would regard her body and reproductive choices as her own, especially in light of past abuses. Yet in the abortion debate we see rhetoric that reflects a deep divide in worldview between those who emphasise 'rights' over and against the 'personhood' of both the unborn child and the two parents.

The Christian understanding of personhood is intimately linked to the central Christian belief that God is one substance but three persons—Father, Son and Holy Spirit, each in relationship with the other.

Christians believe that humans are unique in being created in God's image and as such are relational beings. The implication of this belief is that as individuals we are incomplete, and that our completeness is found in others.

Abortion denies the concept of true personhood to the dependent foetus. It dismisses the child's total dependence on the mother, and the way this dependence wonderfully reflects the human personhood of the baby.

Abortion also denies a Christian concept of personhood to the mother and father of the aborted child. The Christian worldview rejects the idea of the autonomous individual that is foundational to the feminist perspective of 'reproductive rights' of women. Rather, a Christian understanding of what it is to be human suggests that the whole of society is affected by abortion as the person in the womb who is aborted is torn from a matrix of persons-in-relationship that comprises human society. It is for these reasons—the large, orientating and foundational messages about who God is, and who we are as humans, that Christians fall on the side of the debate that they do. This stance does not (or at least should not) deny the intricacies and complexities of individual cases, but at the same time provides compelling reasons for those who adopt a Christian worldview to oppose abortion as a legitimate course of action.

In conclusion, where, by feminist we mean someone who champions the dignity, rights, responsibilities, and glories of women as equal in importance to those of men and who therefore refuses discrimination against women,[27] Christians rightly should be (and have been) partners in the struggle. However where feminism has elevated individual rights above the Lordship of God in our lives, such a partnership breaks down.

The Christian understanding of life celebrates male and female as equal bearers of God's image, but also delights in the difference between the genders—the mutuality and complementarity that each gives the other. At various times some feminists have either literally or effectively rejected males altogether. The creation account in the book of Genesis shows that humanity is somehow incomplete without both male and female in relationship with each other and with God. Feminism's battle to restore something of the equality and complementarity of the original design is in harmony with a Christian vision of life. But when this complex battle becomes a rejection of key societal institutions such as marriage and family, and the community of all people—male and female, feminists move into territory where Christians cannot join them.

RESPONSE

QUeSTiON

1. **What would be a good slogan to sum up the underlying beliefs of Feminism?**

2. **Why do you think 'second wave' feminism occurred when it did?**

3. **How successful has the women's movement been in reaching its goals of equality?**

DiSCUSSiON

A. When does the concept of choice—choice in career, in family, in terms of reproduction —have its limits? At what point does responsibility play a part in rightly limiting our choices?

B. In the struggle for women's rights, what role is there in emphasising the similarity between men and women? When can a focus on the differences between the genders contribute to the same discussion?

C. To what degree do you think Christianity has contributed to the wellbeing of females in the Western world?

D. What is the significance of Jesus' attitude to women in an assessment of the links between feminism and Christianity?

Teenagers are just cavemen and women at heart
By Ellen Connolly *Sydney Morning Herald*, 15 December 2004

After three decades of the feminist revolution, this is where attitudes have evolved to: teenage boys want a future of wealth, sex with many beautiful women, fast cars and sport. Girls dream of romance, a career, meeting Mr Right and shared parenting.

The attitudes are revealed in a study in which 420 Australian students in years 11 and 12 were asked to imagine their futures. The results show continuing gender differences when it comes to careers, housework and childcare, Chilla Bulbeck told the Australian and International Feminisms Conference in Sydney yesterday.

Professor Bulbeck, of the women's studies department at the University of Adelaide, said her study sought to replicate and compare research conducted by Dr Anne Summers in the 1970s.

She concluded that traditional male and female archetypes might be dressed in modern clothes in the young people's essays, but woman the nurturer and man the hunter were not far from the surface.

Her findings also go against 'some young media feminists' claims that gender differences had disappeared'.

Where young women wrote of love, romance and a relationship based on mutual understanding, the young men 'are more focused on their beautiful, sexy, younger, compliant wives and girlfriends, who are sometimes supermodels or Playmates'.

The boys ... dreamt of fame and fortune. Some imagined they were football stars, nightclub owners or singers.

More than 60 per cent of the girls wrote that they would go to university, compared with fewer than 5 per cent in 1970. Career was important to 65 per cent of the girls compared with about 12 per cent in 1970.

Sex and affluence were more important to the boys.

Career was slightly more important to the girls than to the boys. Marriage was important to 70 per cent of the girls—slightly more than in the 1970s study—and a man's earning capacity still matters to some girls.

DiSCUSSiON

E. Are the findings above surprising and what do they tell you about gender relations and the feminist cause?

PeRCEPTiON

1. What appear to you to be the most appealing aspects of feminism as a way of viewing the world?

2. What are its most identifiable weaknesses?

CHAPTER 8

My truth/Your truth

RELATIVISM

John Dickson

> There are many kinds of eyes. Even the Sphinx has eyes – and consequently there are many kinds of 'truths', and consequently there is no truth.
>
> FREDERICK NIETZSCHE[1]

INTRODUCTION

There is an ancient Indian parable in the Buddhist Scriptures, which tells how six blind men were once summoned to inspect an elephant and describe what they could feel. The first at the head declares, 'Sire, an elephant is like a pot'. The second feels the ears and exclaims, 'An elephant is like a winnowing-basket'. Another is led to a leg and insists it is a 'pillar' and the one holding the tail is sure it is a 'brush'. And so on. An argument breaks out over the identity of the object: 'Yes, it is!', 'No, it is not', and so on, till they came to fisticuffs over the matter. The whole thing descends into chaos. Then, reflecting on the parable, the Buddha compares the blind men to the many gurus of India: 'For, quarrelling, each to his view they cling. Such folk see only one side of a thing.'[2]

The point of the parable is that when it comes to matters philosophical, truth is in the eye of the beholder (or, in the case of blind men, the hand of the holder). In other words, your perspective determines your views. A person brought up a Christian will probably see things Christianly; a person brought up a Muslim will probably see things Islamically. One person views abortion as immoral; another views it as perfectly legitimate. No-one is right or wrong. It is just one's perspective or viewpoint.

Philosophers call this approach to life *relativism*. Officially defined, relativism is 'the theory of knowledge or ethics which holds that criteria of judgment are relative, varying with the individual, time, and circumstance'.[3] As a worldview, relativism has impacted the range of human experience—morality, culture, religion, philosophy, science and the very notion of existence itself.

So where did relativism come from? What factors gave rise to this way of looking at life?

HISTORY

The word 'relativism' first appeared in 1859 in the writings of Scottish philosopher Sir William Hamilton. More interesting than the origin of the word is that the idea goes back long, long before the big brains of the nineteenth century.

Protagoras and Plato. Scholars generally agree that the first 'relativist' was the ancient Greek philosopher Protagoras (approximately 490–421 BC). You might remember him from the chapter on Humanism, with which he also has links. Protagoras was a 'Sophist', an itinerant teacher of grammar, literature and philosophy. His book, called simply *Truth,* opened with these words: 'Man is the measure of all things: of the things which are, that they are, and of the things which are not, that they are not.'[4] In other words, what is true and false is determined not by things outside of a person, but simply by a person's own perspective. As he explains later in the book, 'Things are for every man what they seem to him to be'.[5]

Not everyone was happy with old Protagoras. Perhaps no name is more associated with philosophical wisdom than the Athenian intellectual Plato (428–348 BC). Plato provided a devastating critique of Protagoras' idea that 'Man is the measure of all things'. If everything is relative to man's perspective, argued Plato, that must also apply to Protagoras' own idea that truth is relative. If so, his view is just an opinion and so not worth worrying much about. But if Protagoras really thinks it is true that things are only true according to a person's perspective, then, that would mean Protagoras' idea is actually false because at least one truth (Protagoras' idea) would then not be relative.

Most of the world was satisfied with Plato's arguments against Protagoras, and it was two millennia before people started to have another serious go at the relativist idea. Nevertheless, as time rolled on numerous cultural ripples gathered pace and came together to form a wave that many today enjoy riding. Some important 'ripples' in the wave of relativism include the following:

1. Philosophy. The German philosopher Immanuel Kant (1724–1804) argued that the true nature of reality was beyond our human senses. All we can deal with are the phenomena we see, smell, touch and so on. The deeper stuff of life, like God and morality, are inaccessible to our human senses, Kant said. Kant wasn't rejecting these deeper things (which he called 'noumena'). And he certainly wasn't a relativist. But the effect of his philosophy was that people who didn't believe in God and an Absolute moral code started to argue that only things you can see, touch, smell and so on are objectively real; all the other stuff was subjective speculation. Pretty soon, other philosophers were arguing that the 'truths' of spirituality, ethics and culture were simply relative truths—true only within the framework of the society in which they were believed.[6]

2. Anthropology. A major contributor to the wave of relativism was cultural anthropology, the comparative study of human societies. Early anthropologists assumed that Western culture was superior to all others. This assumption began to be challenged, however, by a new breed of anthropologists including the German-born Franz Boas (1858–1942) and the Americans Ruth Benedict (1887–1948) and Margaret Mead (1901–1978). These anthropologists insisted that no-one from one culture has the right to critique another culture. British ways are only 'truths' within British culture and have no relevance for assessing the cultures of, say, Native Americans (studied by Benedict) or Samoans (studied by Mead). In 1947, as the United Nations was developing the Universal Declaration of Human Rights, the American Anthropological Association even issued a statement challenging the whole project, arguing that moral values are relative to individual cultures and should not be thought to apply universally.

A third ripple joined the wave of modern relativism.

3. Psychology. Many suspect that modern psychology played a part in the rise of relativism. A key insight of psychology is that many of our actions and beliefs are determined by patterns of thought that lie beneath the surface of our everyday consciousness (until they are uncovered at a counselling session). A big name here is the German father of psychoanalysis, Sigmund Freud (1856–1939). Among other things, Freud argued that the entire religious sentiment was the result of our infantile longings for a protective father figure and/or a regression to our earliest postnatal feelings of oneness with our mothers. Freud's views were speculative, but he and other early psychologists had a real impact on Western views of religious 'truth'. It could be argued that religion was an internal psychological phenomenon. Not only are religious beliefs social constructs ('true' only relative within a communal framework), they are psychological constructs as well ('true' only within the framework of the believer's mind). This relativising of beliefs to a psychological process seemed to establish Relativism itself as the grand Truth to which all other 'truths' had to bow.

TESTING THE CLAIMS OF RELATIVISM

A diversity of truth claims in a pluralist setting is affirmed by relativism, yet such a claim frequently bumps up against (or smashes into) real life in a way that makes it hard to sustain.

The New York Times editorial shortly after the September 11 attacks admitted that the event shook the foundations of intellectual belief in the subjective nature of truth and ethical judgments:

'Such assertions seem peculiar when trying to account for the recent attack. The destruction seems to cry out for a transcendent ethical perspective. Even mild relativism seems troubling by contrast.'[7]

CENTRAL BELIEFS

The three spheres of relativism

Once the wave of relativism got moving it swamped all before it: the catchphrase 'Everything is relative' sounds almost trendy in some circles today. And while few of us really believe that *everything* is relative, there are at least three spheres of life that have come to be viewed relativistically: culture, morals and religion.

1. Cultural relativism is the view that no one culture is better or worse than another—just as the early anthropologists argued. The habits of one culture are true/valid *only within that culture* and are not necessarily true/valid for another culture. Let me give you a striking example of the way a hard-core relativist would argue. Female circumcision (the removal of the clitoris, usually of a teenage girl) is considered a noble tradition in Somali culture. However, in the West many condemn the practice as 'female mutilation'. A relativist stance on this issue insists that neither the Somali approval of female circumcision nor the Western disapproval of female circumcision is right in an ultimate sense. These viewpoints are both correct *within the cultural framework* in which they are held. Female circumcision is *right for* Somalis and *wrong for* Westerners.

In Australia in 2006 the Egyptian Muslim cleric Sheikh Taj el-Din al Hilali was quoted comparing unveiled women to 'uncovered meat' inviting the attacks of prowling cats (meaning men). The uproar in the media was fascinating. While apologising for the offence to non-Muslim Australians, Sheik Hilali defended his comments on the grounds that they were intended for a Muslim audience. For Muslims, he believed, his teachings were culturally appropriate. Not good enough, declared Sophie Mirabella MP, who took the opportunity in Parliament to call for an end to this relativising of cultural values:

I think we do live in an age where we have slid too far into relativism, and there must be some absolutes in our society.

AUSTRALIAN PRIME MINISTER JOHN HOWARD

(Speaking against a bill to allow therapeutic cloning for embryonic stem cell research).

We are not going to stand by and let this man get away with it. There needs to be an end to cultural relativism ... There are basic laws that apply to all Australians and one Australian legal system should apply to every single Australian whether they be atheist, Christian or Muslim.[8]

2. Moral relativism is the same logic applied to the question of right and wrong. For one person abortion is immoral; for another it is perfectly legitimate. No-one is right or wrong. Such views can only be evaluated relative to the framework of the person holding such views. A fascinating example of a thoroughgoing relativist is Lord Bertrand Russell (1872–1970), probably the greatest atheistic mind of the twentieth century. In 1948 Russell was invited to debate, live on BBC radio, the renowned Roman Catholic philosopher, Frederick Copleston (1907–1994). At one point, Copleston pressed Russell to explain what he thought was the basis of distinguishing right from wrong. Specifically, he raises the example of the behaviour of the Commandant of Belsen Concentration Camp during Hitler's Nazi rule. Russell admitted that, for him, choosing morality is just like choosing one colour from another.

Copleston: Yes, but what's your justification for distinguishing between good and bad or how do you view the distinction between them?

Russell: I don't have any justification any more than I have when I distinguish between blue and yellow. What is my justification for distinguishing between blue and yellow? I can see they are different.

Copleston: Granted. But there's no objective criterion outside feeling then for condemning the conduct of the Commandant of Belsen, in your view?

Russell: No more than there is for the colour-blind person who's in exactly the same state. Why do we intellectually condemn the colour-blind man? Isn't it because he's in the minority?[9]

For the relativist, what is right and wrong comes down to the feeling of the majority. That's all there is. The Christian worldview, by contrast, insists that the world was created by God and so reality is shaped by his own character (of justice, love, and so on). Ethics, then, are not a matter of feeling or democracy; they derive objectively from the One who stands at the centre of the universe. More about that later.

3. Religious relativism is the view that religious claims are not true in any external way, but only within the belief system of the religious adherent. So, for instance, while it is true for Christians that God became a man in Jesus Christ and died on a cross,[10] it is true for Muslims that Jesus did not die on a cross and was only a human being.[11] No-one is right or wrong in an ultimate sense. Both groups are right about Jesus relative to their own religious framework. Such religious relativism is sometimes called simply 'pluralism', the view that religious truth is plural in form, not singular.

A modern version of the Buddhist Elephant parable is offered by a leading pluralist today, Professor John Hick of the University of Birmingham (UK). He presents us with a picture first used in early studies of illusion:[12]

The sketch, as you can see, shows an ambiguous figure drawn to look like both a duck (facing left) and a rabbit (facing right). Take a moment to see both for yourself. If shown to a culture that knew ducks but not rabbits, says Hick, the picture will be interpreted quite validly as a sketch of a duck. If shown to a culture that knew only rabbits, however, the picture would be interpreted naturally enough as that of a rabbit. No-one is right or wrong, says Hick. It is simply a matter of perception. Likewise with religion, Hick argues. Muslims see Allah, Hindus see Vishnu, Krishna and so on, and Christians see Jesus. No-one's belief is true in an ultimate sense; but everyone's belief is true relative to their cultural framework.

CONTACT AND DEPARTURE FROM CHRISTIANITY

John Hick's Duck-Rabbit analogy wonderfully illustrates not just religious relativism but cultural and moral relativism as well. Somalis see female circumcision as a noble practice; Westerners see it as mutilation. Pro-choicers see abortion as a woman's right; pro-lifer's see it is as the murder of a helpless human being. No-one is right or wrong; it is just 'ducks' and 'rabbits'. We just see life differently. That's all.

Or is it?

1. The presumption of relativism. The Duck-Rabbit sketch unwittingly reveals a hidden assumption of relativists. In reality, the picture is not a sketch of a rabbit, or of a duck. It is a sketch deliberately drawn to look like *both* a duck and a rabbit. The unknowing subjects in the experiment might be justified in seeing either a duck or a rabbit, but the person showing the picture, the one conducting the experiment, knows full well this is a clever work of art designed to trick people. What does this say about the relativist? Well, for one thing, it reveals that the relativist is claiming implicitly to know something that the others do not: he or she apparently knows that people do not view things absolutely but only partially or relatively. Relativism, in other words, claims to be able to see the whole picture, while the rest of us see ducks and rabbits. Actually, this is exactly the point of Buddha's Elephant Parable, and he had the honesty to admit it. The Hindu gurus of India were blind to the total reality, whereas the Buddha knew the Truth. Whenever relativists say, 'Each person has their own truth—it's all relative', they are presuming to know there is an 'elephant' beyond the 'pot'. And they never stop to tell us how they know this.

2. Self-refutation. A major problem with relativism is the one Plato raised almost two and a half thousand years ago. Relativism is self-contradictory. You cannot claim that truth is relative and expect people to accept what you say as 'true'. If the statement is true absolutely, it proves that not everything is true relatively. And, if the statement is only relatively true, we can dismiss it as an opinion.

If it is *true* that truth is relative, there is automatically one truth that is not relative (the truth of relativism). And, if you allow this exception, it's going to be very difficult to disallow other exceptions. And then the whole relativism wave crashes. Philosophers call this the 'exemption problem'.

'CREED' BY STEVE TURNER

We believe in Marxfreuddarwin

We believe everything is OK

As long as you don't hurt anyone,

To the best of your definition of hurt

And to the best of your knowledge.

We believe in sex before during and after marriage.

We believe in the therapy of sin.

We believe that adultery is fun.

We believe that sodomy's OK

We believe that taboos are taboo.

We believe that everything's getting better

despite evidence to the contrary.

The evidence must be investigated.

You can prove anything with evidence.

We believe there's something in horoscopes,

UFO's and bent spoons;

Jesus was a good man just like Buddha

Mohammed and ourselves.
He was a good moral teacher although we think
his good morals were bad.

We believe that all religions are basically the same,
at least the one we read was.

They all believe in love and goodness.

They only differ on matters of creation sin heaven hell God and salvation.

We believe that man is essentially good.

It's only his behaviour that lets him down.

This is the fault of society.

Society is the fault of conditions.

Conditions are the fault of society.

We believe that each man must find the truth

that is right for him

Reality will adapt accordingly.

The universe will readjust.
History will alter.

We believe that there is no absolute truth

Excepting the truth that there is no absolute truth.

We believe in the rejection of creeds.[13]

3. Relativism and tolerance. Probably the most attractive thing about relativism for the average person on the street is the seeming connection between relativism and tolerance. If I insist that moral, cultural and religious 'truths' are simply relative—that no-one is right or wrong—then this is likely to inspire tolerance toward other people's views. And God knows we need more tolerance today!

This longing for tolerance is one thing the Christian worldview shares with the relativist. But before we decide that tolerance is best won through relativism it might be worth asking what we mean by tolerance. For many today, tolerance is little more than a willingness to accept every viewpoint as true and valid. But I want to suggest this is not tolerance at all, but simply a strategy for avoiding arguments. True tolerance does not involve accepting every viewpoint as true and valid; it involves treating with love and humility someone whose opinions you believe to be untrue and invalid. A tolerant pro-lifer, to give just one example, is not one who accepts as true and valid the pro-choice idea that it is okay to kill unwanted foetuses. No: the tolerant pro-lifer is one who, while rejecting abortionist arguments, nonetheless treats pro-choicers with kindness and respect. True tolerance is the noble ability to treat with grace those with whom you disagree. For Christians this ought to be second nature, since the Lord proclaimed in the Christian gospel, is the epitome of humility, love and gentleness.

RELATIVIST DINNER PARTY

JANE: So Rob, how's your work for Vision of the World going?

ROB: I've just come back from Africa. It's going alright, but it gets pretty depressing at times. The amount of kids who are AIDS orphans is unbelievable. And you know really, when it comes down to it, it's so preventable. Fidelity or condoms will do the trick. Not to mention the drugs that the West could provide.

GARRY: Hard to tell people how to live their lives though, isn't it? I mean, monogamy's just not part of the culture is it? Who are we to judge?

ROB: I guess. I just think about the kids though eh? It's really tragic. And these poor women who get it. It's not their fault.

FELICITY: Yeah Rob that must be tough. But I'm really conscious of not imposing our values onto anyone else. I mean how about that Christian politician banging on about therapeutic cloning for stem cell research on the news this week. Talk about living in the dark ages. How can she be so arrogant? Trying to stop legitimate medical research for the sake of her make-believe religion.

ROB: It's a complicated issue. I don't think you have to be religious to have your doubts about that one.

JORDAN: But Rob, what right do others have to tell us how to live? I mean really! We don't all see the world in the same way.

FELICITY: It's the twenty-first century for goodness sake. Anyone with half a brain or a conscience understands that we have to accept that what's right for you, may not be OK for me. We have to respect that. Appealing to some god, or the Bible or whatever fairytale you happen to like doesn't allow for tolerance. And without tolerance we might as well be back in the cave.

GARRY: Speaking of the cave. How about those gang rapists trying to appeal their sentences? I reckon they should increase them.

FELICITY: Absolutely! Lock 'em up for life I say. They don't deserve to see the light of day again.

JANE: No arguments about that one.

JORDAN: More Champagne anyone?

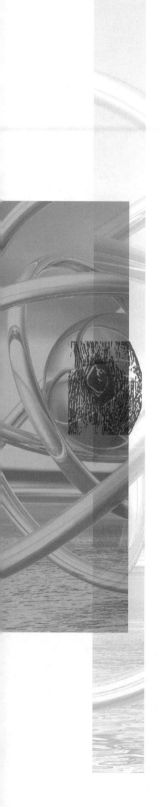

4. To what are things 'relative'? At the heart of
relativism is the insistence that 'truths' are only
true relative to a framework. The 'truths' of Jesus'
deity and death, for example, are true only relative
to the framework of Christianity (they are not true
relative to the framework of Islam). The concern
of relativism is to connect beliefs with their bases.
Female circumcision has a basis only in reference to
Somali culture. Morals have a basis only in reference
to the society in which they are agreed upon. And so
on. Admittedly, there is a truth here that relativists
have highlighted: our beliefs must depend upon
a framework; they must have a reference point.
Otherwise, they are just random shots in the dark.
This is a dangerous truth for relativists to uncover,
for the question that comes immediately to mind
is: upon what framework does relativism depend?
Or, to what reference point does relativism refer?
The answer is: none, except within the mind of the
relativist.

The question of a reference point is one that presents
itself to all claims about the world, whether scientific,
moral, cultural or religious. In other words, every
claim must have a basis. When traditional Somalis
claim that it is a noble thing to circumcise a teenage
girl they must, in a multicultural society like ours,
be able to provide reasons why the practice is
acceptable. Otherwise, they cannot complain when
Westerners protest, 'This custom is a violation
of women's rights!'. Of course, it is also true that
Westerners must, likewise, provide reasons for their
protestation. The reasons will indicate the reference
point or framework. So, for instance, Westerners
might try to put forward medical, sociological
and psychological arguments against female
circumcision. But if it turned out that there were
no reasons for the respective views, beyond saying
'this is what our culture thinks', then neither side of
the debate would have any firm basis for critiquing
the other. A kind of resigned relativism would then
be advisable. My point is simple. If our views can

be shown to correspond to more than the whims of human culture and mind, relativism loses its footing (if it had any) and relevance.

This is not the chapter for outlining the basis of the Christian worldview but the larger point is worth pondering. Christians have reasons for thinking there is a God to whom we all belong. They have reasons for thinking God has revealed himself in the teaching, miracles, death and resurrection of Jesus Christ. And they have reasons for thinking the Bible is God's Word to humanity. Once persuaded of these things, Christians find comfort in the fact that their views are not determined by culture, tradition or psychological make-up. They live and think in accordance with the Absolute—an Absolute who has revealed himself on the human stage. This comfort is something relativism has no possibility of replicating.

RESPONSE QUeSTiON

1. What would be a good slogan to sum up the underlying beliefs of Relativism?

2. What is your response to the arguments of Anthropology that 'truths' within one culture have no relevance to assessing the values of other cultures? Do you detect limitations to this argument?

3. What value do you see in a definition of tolerance that involves 'treating with love and humility someone whose opinions you believe to be untrue and invalid' (page 184)? Is this the version of tolerance you come across in daily life?

DiSCUSSiON

A. How do you explain the way relativism has become so pervasive and popular in our society?

B. The strength of relativism (in theory at least) is its willingness to acknowledge the vast array of perspectives that different people have when they look at the world. What are the limitations of such a stance? Where do you personally draw the line in terms of being able to say another person's outlook and actions are legitimate and justified?

RELATIVISING OURSELVES TO DEATH

Sir Arnold Toynbee was a famous historian who in the 1940s wrote a massive study on the rise and fall of world civilisations. He based his study on twenty-one world civilisations—ranging from ancient Rome to imperial China, from Babylon to the Aztecs. Toynbee found that great societies are seldom simply overrun by some other civilisation. Rather, they commit a kind of cultural suicide. Toynbee located a series of characteristics that he claimed were typical of societies in decline.

One of these characteristics he said, was a promiscuity, which Toynbee meant not so much in the sexual sense, but as the indiscriminate acceptance of anything and everything, an unfocused eclecticism and uncritical tolerance. Toynbee described this promiscuity as 'an act of self-surrender to the melting pot ... in Religion and Literature and Language and Art as well as ... Manners and Customs', the triumph of a mass mind.[14]

DISCUSSION

C. What danger do you perceive in an uncritical tolerance of everything?

D. Is such a thing applicable to our society?

PeRCEPTiON

1. What appear to you to be the most appealing aspects of Relativism as a way of viewing the world?

2. What are its most identifiable weaknesses?

NEW AGE

CHAPTER 9
Do-it-yourself
NEW AGE SPIRITUALITY

Ross Clifford

INTRODUCTION

> My intention for your experience of religion is that it becomes a religion of the self.
>
> RON SMOTHERMON[1]

At a recent stay in hospital I got talking to Jillian, a young medical technician. She introduced herself and, while hooking me up to a variety of machines, commented on the 'Simpsons' t-shirt I was wearing. Obviously a fan of the show, she asked whether I had seen the episode where Lisa explores Buddhism. Lisa finds herself torn, with Christmas approaching she still wants to be caught up in all the traditional Christian activities. 'That episode describes me', said Jillian.

'I am searching for something more, I'm open to the supernatural but I'm fascinated by all religions, not just Christianity. I'm exploring Wicca and I love crystals. I guess I'm New Age, if that is the right term.' New Age was an appropriate nametag for

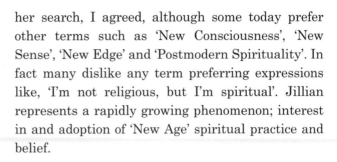

her search, I agreed, although some today prefer other terms such as 'New Consciousness', 'New Sense', 'New Edge' and 'Postmodern Spirituality'. In fact many dislike any term preferring expressions like, 'I'm not religious, but I'm spiritual'. Jillian represents a rapidly growing phenomenon; interest in and adoption of 'New Age' spiritual practice and belief.

HISTORY

The New Age movement has no founder-figure like Jesus or Buddha. It has no church, authoritative text like the Bible, or agreed prayer book. It is an evolving spiritual movement. However, as we will see shortly, we can pinpoint the emergence of the phenomenon from the late twentieth century. It is a new religious movement, but this is not to say it didn't have forebears. In the late nineteenth/ early twentieth century, there were 'magical' and spiritual movements looking for a new way, or a means of ushering in an Aquarian age.[3] For example, in 1875 Madame Blavatsky (1831–1891) established the Theosophical Society, which drew on the hidden insights of Buddhist, Hindu and Western occult traditions so as to examine the nature of God. Although theosophical traditions in the West can be traced back to the Renaissance, Blavatsky's inspiration was a modern forerunner for New Age.

Charles Leadbeater (1854–1934) was a leading Theosophist who served as the first bishop of the liberal Catholic Church in Australia. Dr Greg Tillett states, 'The modern occult revival owes more to him than to anyone else; his concepts and ideas; his popularising of occult and theosophical terms and principles run through all modern works on these subjects ...Words like *karma*, *chakra* ... have continued to be used in the sense in which he used them ...'.[4]

Another influenced by the Theosophical Society was the architect Walter Burleigh Griffin (1876–

1937). His use of the esoteric craft of geomancy (a belief that there are lines of energy—ley lines —that traverse the planet that create harmonious space and atmosphere is evident in his design of Australia's capital city, Canberra.[5]

With respect to movements like Wicca, it is often asked if we can go back further than the last hundred years or so to discover its origins. After all, forms of witchcraft, magic and sorcery are found in biblical times, in medieval history and primal cultures. Certainly there is some connection with these old 'pagan' ideas, however New Age and Wicca have distinctly reshaped practices like astrology and nature-based spirituality for the seeker of today. Novels such as Dan Brown's *The Da Vinci Code* transport the reader back to Goddess ideas of biblical times and Gnostic movements with initiation into secret teachings, sometimes about Jesus, but New Age faith has evolved well beyond these early influences.[6]

Personalities

Watching talk-show host Oprah Winfrey is often an encounter with New Age thought. Leaders of the movement like Deepak Chopra and Marianne Williamson are regular guests.[7] Hollywood stars are attracted to this spirituality. Actress Shirley MacLaine was one who led the way.[8] Others quickly followed, exploring a mix of Kabbalah and Scientology. Australian pop star Fiona Horne is a leading Wiccan.

However, New Age is a people movement, not just Hollywood directed. Leading consumer-predictor, Faith Popcorn states that everyday people will continue to develop personalised faiths (DIY religion) by blending parts of belief systems and rituals. She concludes, 'Customised Bibles will be created, merging passages from Animism to Zen'.[9] The personalities of New Age are our next door neighbours, teachers, friends and colleagues.

Charmed (TV series) 1998 – 2006

The long running TV series *Charmed* is a good example of interest in Witchcraft, which itself is a function of New Age thinking. After premiering with the episode *Something Wicca this way*, the series lasted for eight seasons and captured the devotion of millions of viewers.

The plot involved three sisters who were powerful 'good witches' each with a unique supernatural ability. Together they battled demons and forces of darkness in San Francisco. In season three one of the sisters, Prue, was killed by a demon only to be replaced by a previously unknown half-sister, Paige. The action of the show involved ouija boards, sacred bonds, levitation, astral projection, telekinesis (moving objects with your mind), molecular combustion and ancient prophecies.

In its depiction of characters having led previous lives, death ushering in a state of disembodied afterlife and being neither good nor evil but inevitable, the program reflected some widely held New Age beliefs.

INFLUENCE

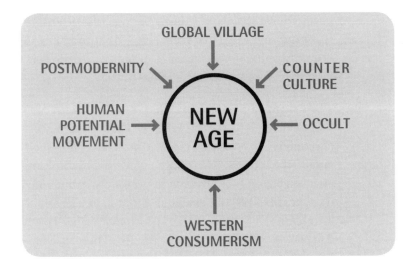

The above chart reveals that in the last 30 or 40 years a number of developments and forces of change have created an environment where the New Age movement has flourished. Lets look at each of these areas in more detail, whilst acknowledging that this is not an absolute statement on origins.

We are a **global village.** Via the media, immigration and travel, Western societies are increasingly coming into direct contact with the spiritual traditions of the East such as Buddhism and Taoism. Hindu gurus like Swami Muktanda have brought Siddha Yoga to the West.

In the 1960s and early 1970s baby boomers rebelled against institutions and traditional ways. Lifestyle alternatives were explored, and some experimented with drugs and Eastern religions. The New Age movement is the 'heir' to the 1960s **counterculture.**[10]

Occult means the secret, esoteric or hidden things. Since the 1970s various occult traditions and practices have prospered, although they have been with us throughout human history. Spiritual seekers have in particular been drawn to practices of divination such as tarot and astrology. Also, people often do religion today as they shop. They purchase goods from a variety of shops and give little attention to brand loyalty. This **Western Consumerism** is seen in spirituality where the 'customer' doesn't want to be limited to one shop or brand.

The **human potential movement,** with its emphasis on attaining personal 'peak experiences' through techniques like mind powers, has flourished since the 1970s. Proponents of this thinking encourage you to learn how to positively script your own destiny relying on your mind and thoughts. The leaders of the movement include Wayne Dyer, Anthony Robbins and Werner Erhard. This emphasis fits well with an often-held New Age affirmation that you are the master of your own destiny.

Finally there is **postmodernity.** A chapter on this worldview is included in this book, and it has a direct relationship to New Age. Many postmoderns see the stories of modernity, which rely on science and technology, as very limiting. Therefore they look to myth, if not supernatural experiences, for stories that transcend science and technology.[11]

The growth of the New Age has been assisted by **other factors.** Undoubtedly one of these is a lack of trust in such institutions as the Church. Institutionalised religion is often viewed as oppressing women and their spirituality, as well as having a history of sexual and other abuse. These concerns are certainly found in Wicca, which endeavours to bring a balance to what is felt to be a lopsided 'patriarchal' view of God as a male. Also numerous seekers are looking for a healing spirituality in the midst of our chaotic world. Wicca, like its umbrella movement New Age, offers 'magic' on behalf of others and oneself, for healing, as one aligns oneself with alternative reality.[12]

CENTRAL BELIEFS

New Age is not primarily a set of commandments and beliefs. Its heartbeat is: 'I want an inner life; I want to commune with nature and humanity; I want to find out why I'm here.' It is therefore difficult to list its beliefs. Having said that, it certainly does have two marks. *One* is that it is eclectic in nature. That means it will draw on numerous religious traditions and practices. It's okay to consult the stars, wear a cross, rely on a crystal and try Buddhist meditation. In contrast, the Bible is the sole authority for what Christians believe and it is their source for what is right and wrong. *A second mark* of New Age is its emphasis on self-spirituality. In a populist sense this is found in the self-help teaching of media giants like Oprah Winfrey. It's about self-discovery, progress and growth, with the individual to decide how that is done.[14] This is a real mark of a DIY religion with each seeker believing they are empowered to 'create' a faith that meets their own needs and aspirations. Neville Drury states, 'One should transform oneself before endeavouring to transform others.'[15]

Whilst one must be cautious in listing New Age beliefs, aspects of it can be contrasted with the Christian worldview.

GOD

Not all New Agers believe in God. Fiona Horne acknowledges that for Wicca god can exist within the individual, but not in the sky out of reach. However she concludes, 'I have always felt gods and goddesses do not exist in their own right but are projections of our consciousness'.[16] Most speak of god in a pantheistic and monist way. In a simplistic sense this can be thus expressed: all is one = monism; since all is one, all is divine = pantheism.

The great refrain running throughout the New Age, is that we malfunction because we have been indoctrinated, or ... been "brainwashed" by mainstream society and culture. The mores of the established order – its materialism, its competitiveness, together with the importance it attaches to playing roles – are held to disrupt what it is to be authentically human.

PAUL HEELAS[13]

MONISM + PANTHEISM = NEW AGE GOD

This sense that all is one, all is divine and that we ourselves have eternally been part of this divine energy, is well expressed by one of the characters in the best selling New Age novel, *The Celestine Prophecy:*

> I sat down again on the rock, and again, everything seemed close; the rugged outcrop on which I was sitting, the tall trees further down the slope and the other mountains on the horizon. And as I watched the limbs of the trees sway gently in the breeze, I experienced not just a visual perception of the event, but a physical sensation as well, as if the limbs moving in the wind were hairs on my body.

> I perceived everything to be somehow part of me. As I sat on the peak of the mountain looking out at the landscape falling away from me in all directions, it felt exactly as if what I had always known as my physical body was only the head of a much larger body consisting of everything else I could see. I experienced the entire universe looking out on itself through my eyes.

> This perception induced a flash of memory. My mind raced backward in time, past the beginning of my trip to Peru, past my childhood and my birth. The realisation was present that my life did not, in fact, begin with conception and birth on this planet. It began much earlier with the formation of the rest of me, my real body, the universe itself.[17]

Here we see a stunning example of the *New Age* sense of oneness of the self with the universe. You may be able to detect a sharp contrast with Christianity at this point. While holding to the immanence of God and that through the Holy Spirit the 'divine' resides within the followers of Jesus, Christian thinking asserts that God is also separate or distinct from us. God is the creator of all things, and he alone exists eternally (Genesis 1 and 2). He is also a personal God, more than energy and consciousness.

However, as we have already mentioned, not all New Agers are pantheistic. Some will hold to a more personal God, others will be interested in 'first-nation' beliefs, such as the beliefs of indigenous people like the dreamtime of Australian aboriginals.

CREATURES DISTINCT

Christian philosopher Francis Schaeffer liked to point out that in Michelangelo's famous painting of God creating Adam in the Sistine chapel—God's finger never touches Adam's.

Schaeffer said this was deliberate on the part of the artist who understood that Adam was not an overflow of God's being—not made from the 'stuff' of God but like all humanity was distinct from God, created by God but not of the essence of God.[18]

This is in marked contrast to the New Age Spirituality's monism and pantheism and idea that everything partakes of the divine essence.

The apostle Paul's letter to the church in Rome speaks about the pagan world and its misplaced reverence of the creation: 'They exchanged the truth of God for a lie, and worshipped and served created things rather than the Creator who is forever praised. Amen' (Romans 1:25).

SELF

As mentioned, there is a strong sense of our own divinity, as all is one and all is divine. A key outworking of this is that it is *you and me* who are in control of our lives. For example, a friend of mine was at University and frustrated with his studies and parents. He took a Mind Powers course that taught him that he could 'change the script'. He alone was responsible for what was occurring in his life. And he did change the script. He set things right with his parents and changed his attitude to his studies. Salvation, he was taught, is ultimately about discovering our self, our own divinity and controlling our own destiny. Jesus' affirmation, 'I and the Father (the divine) are One' is held to be true for all of us (John 10:30).

In contrast, Christianity affirms the human dignity and worth of all humanity, not because we are part of the Godhead, but as a consequence of God's love for his creation. Despite recognising the importance of taking responsibility for our own actions, Christian understanding is that God's will for us, and external factors beyond our control are significant elements of the play of life.

THE FRUITLESS SEARCH FOR THE STRENGTH WITHIN

Michele, a Christian believer, recalls a moment when the inadequacies of New Age came sharply into focus. It was during a time when she had been hospitalised for depression. In a support group with other sufferers, a 'chaplain' who was into a fusion of Buddhism and New Age spirituality, was urging those in the group to look within themselves to find the spiritual strength to overcome their condition. Michele saw this as well-meaning but misguided advice. 'I knew at that point that if I had to find the strength within, I was going to be hopelessly lost', she says. 'I had nothing to give. At my lowest point, I took strength spiritually only from what could come from outside me.'

JESUS

I am attracted to the figure of Jesus – to his
compassion, his courage, his fear, his humanity,
the way he is born and dies, journeys through the
underworld and lives again like Osiris in Egypt,
like the great heroes of mythology. Yet Christianity
requires a leap of faith of such magnitude that I feel
I must parcel up all reason and leave it on the far
side of some rocky gorge.[19]

SAMANTHA TRENOWETH
(Typifies new agers' mixed feelings about Jesus)

New Spirituality seekers are attracted to the person
of Jesus. He is an important spiritual guide who
modelled how we are all one with the Father. He is
not a saviour from sin as we are essentially good.
A Course in Miracles purports to be teachings of
Jesus channelled through a contemporary author.
It states, 'No one is punished for their sins and the
Sons of God are not sinners'.[20]

Jesus is often portrayed as one who travelled and
his wisdom was therefore global. During his missing
years, between the age of 13 and 29 on which the
Bible is silent, Jesus was teaching and studying in
lands such as India, Kashmir, Nepal and Tibet.[21]

In contrast Christianity teaches that Jesus is
uniquely divine, that he did die and rise again to pay
for our sins and his wisdom comes from his divinity,
not his travels.

GUIDANCE

Whilst there is real appreciation for sacred texts and
books on practical spirituality, guidance essentially
lies within us. In the new age, spirituality, the source
of all strength needs to come from within. While
there will be some people who feel good about that,
many are uneasy about such a dynamic and don't

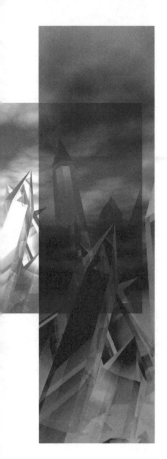

feel they possess all within them that is required for making their way in the world and making sense of life. In contrast to New Age belief about guidance, evangelical Christianity stands for the Bible as the primary source for guidance on morals, life and practice.

New Age devotees who are attracted to occult links will explore 'psychotechnologies' like astrology, tarot cards, yoga, numerology, and *feng shui* (ancient Chinese folk religious practice of placing objects in such a way to promote good fortune by ensuring cosmic energy that flows through the natural world is not blocked), to assist them in their decision-making and guidance for life. In doing so they are rejecting a naturalistic exploration of the cosmos and returning to some of the pre-modern 'ancient' supernatural practices. Christians believe such technologies are unnecessary, as through the Bible and prayer we have a direct connection with God. Further, the Bible warns that such 'psychotechnologies' can unintentionally open one up to dark forces (Deuteronomy 18:9–13). New Age itself, does not believe in the existence of cosmic demonic forces, however some do acknowledge the place of 'dark' angels.

FUTURE

A common New Spirituality belief is reincarnation, which literally means to come again in the flesh. For Hindus and Buddhists, reincarnation takes place between all forms of life including animal life. (For Buddhists there is no soul and one reincarnates in the same way that one candle may be lit by another.) In the West, reincarnation tends to imply that your soul, upon death, transmigrates from your present human life to your next human life in an upward evolutionary spiral. Where one is on the evolutionary spiral depends on the law of karma: what you sow in life you reap.

In contrast Christianity holds to resurrection of the body (1 Corinthians 15). Resurrection implies that you die once (Hebrews 9:27) and your eternal destiny is not lived separate from some bodily experience. In Judaism and Christianity the body is good because God created it. New Age thought is more along the lines of Greek philosophy and Eastern religions that regard the body as inferior to spiritual things, and therefore should be left behind.

Many New Age advocates proclaim a dawning of the Age of Aquarius, which is an era of universal brotherhood. This vision of a transformed cosmos is one of the environment and humanity in harmony, a seamless fabric. For some it is returning to the myth of the lost continent of Atlantis. Christianity has a similar vision, but its climax is dependent on the return of Jesus Christ (Revelation 21–22).

'You are a spiritual being. You are energy, and energy cannot be recreated or destroyed—it just changes form. Therefore the pure essence of you has always been and always will be.'

RHONDA BYRNE
(The Secret)

IMPACT

Afterlife research

Surveys in the US suggest that one in five people believe in reincarnation, while in the UK it is 30–35 percent of the population.[22]

Despite the fact that at census time the majority of Australians tick boxes that indicate allegiance to mainstream religions, such as Christianity and Islam, their lifestyles and spiritual practices often indicate something else. Academic David Tacey has aptly captured the social impact of New Spirituality:

As the masculinist pubs, churches, convents, and barber shops go broke or close down in Australian cities, New Age bookshops and 'awareness centres' are popping up everywhere, offering the public a broad range of largely non-Christian, non-patriarchal esoteric arts and sciences, such as astrology, tarot, I Ching, karma sutra, sacred sex, herbalism, naturopathy, meditation, yoga, psychic massage, channelling, neo-paganism and wicca, martial arts, reincarnation, Eastern religions and philosophies, Native American vision quests and goddess spirituality.[23]

One has only to visit the magazine rack, self-help and religious sections of the local bookshop to appreciate this influence. The astonishing success of Rhonda Byrne's book *The Secret* is further evidence of the growing appeal of New Age teaching.

Read about it

A quick scan of the new age section of any major bookstore will give some indication of the interest in New Age thinking. The titles you are likely to come across include such as the following:

Discover the psychic in you

Cracking the Symbol code

Essential psychic healing

Discover your destiny

Divine guidance

Contacting the spirit world

Leaving the body – a complete guide to astral projection

Advanced Chakra healing

Your sixth sense

media

When I conduct school seminars I find extraordinary interest in topics like Wicca, séances and astral travel (entering a trance or sleep-like state where one's spirit is free to leave the body and journey into other dimensions). Students share their stories of personal involvement. Anna for example, found her dabbling in astral travel had led to a situation where she could not control the 'spirit' guide who accompanied her. She was led into dark experiences.

Also some schools, including Christian schools, have unwittingly used programs to improve students self-esteem that are based on New Age insights including a combination of mind powers and astral travel. In tertiary studies such as nursing and beautician courses there are institutions that advocate techniques such as reiki and therapeutic touch (premised on the notion that there is a unifying cosmic energy—all is one—that can be tapped into and channelled).

Where New Age finds a voice

New Age finds a place in psychology, the natural sciences, health and well-being alternative medicine, in science fiction. In George Lucas' *Star Wars* series the divine energy—the force—carries with it both good and evil like the Hindu Brahman.[26]

The thoughts of the guru Yoda are typical of what we witness in the film:

'Size matters not. Look at me. Judge me by my size, do you? Hmm? Hmm. And well you should not. For my ally is the Force, and a powerful ally it is. Life creates it, makes it grow. Its energy surrounds us and binds us. Luminous beings are we, not this crude matter. You must feel the Force around you; here, between you, me, the tree, the rock, everywhere, yes. Even between the land and the ship.'[27]

(Yoda)

CONTACT AND DEPARTURE FROM CHRISTIANITY

New Age and Christianity do have things in common. There is the belief that life is more than a good job and chasing the dollar. There is openness to the supernatural. For example, the belief in angels is widespread and books and calendars abound on angelic beings from both New Age and Christian authors and artists. There is acceptance of 'divine' guidance. And most importantly there is awareness of our inner ache for divine connection and redemption. There is an understanding that when I tell you my story, you are listening to your own story. There is a search for healing, rescue from harmful ways and transformation. The popularity of Tolkien's *Lord of the Rings* and C.S.Lewis' *The Chronicles of Narnia* show how we connect to myths that embrace such longings.

In their purest forms both Christianity and New Age have a commitment to the environment. GAIA is the name of the ancient Greek goddess of the earth. This is why many New Agers refer to the world as 'Mother Earth'. GAIA is being dedicated to mother earth and she must be preserved, as she is a living entity to whom we are connected. Christianity also affirms our stewardship of creation (Genesis 1). The psalmists declare that the trees, sun, seas, mountains, stars and birds join in the dance of praise to God (Psalms 96, 98 and 148). Romans 8:22 announces the whole of creation groans for the healing of the earth. In both worldviews the environment is important. However in Christianity God alone is the creator and we are his creation, given responsibility for each other and the environment.

Although the primary focus of New Age is on oneself and personal transformation, the most significant departure is the nature of God. In Christianity God is personal, loving, and capable of emotions. He is not just energy or consciousness. Also God, in his nature, is greater than and separate from us. This means salvation is not about finding our own personal divinity, it is about having a lasting friendship with the Creator who is the Lord of our lives and of creation.

Jesus in Christianity is both man and God. In New Age he is only god in the sense that we are all gods. In Christianity he is uniquely God. The divinity of Christ is verified by his resurrection (John 20: 24–29). Anyone who eternally defeats our universal enemy, death, deserves to be worshipped. The resurrection of Jesus is presented as an historical fact with eyewitness verification in trustworthy documents and is not a myth or a secret teaching.[28] However, the Jesus of history answers all the longings found in myths. Tolkien said, 'The (New Testament) gospels contain ... a story of a larger kind which embraces all the essence of fairy stories ... There is no tale that men would rather find was

true, and none which so many sceptical men have accepted as true on its merits ... Legend and history have fused.'[29]

In Tim Winton's novel *Cloudstreet* one of the characters reflects on the alleged difference between himself and a recently convicted criminal. The character confesses his own failings, 'I could've turned out angry and cold like him ... But it's not us and them anymore. It's us and us and us. It's always us. That's what they never tell you. Geez, Rose, I just want to do right. But there's no monsters, only people like us. Funny, but it hurts'. In Christianity we all fail, we all sin, a concept New Age rejects. The implication of the New Age worldview is that there is no saviour for our sins. To adopt the Christian worldview is to appreciate that Jesus died on the cross for our sins. Salvation is not about me, but about what Jesus did for me. The implication of this is that in Jesus I receive liberating grace —forgiveness (John 3:16).

I was watching a television chat program where the interviewer was asking the guest, who was a bishop of a church, a lot of fascinating questions about his life and the people he had met and helped. Finally the interviewer asked the bishop, 'When I die will Jesus interview me, will he ask me any questions?'. 'Oh yes', responded the bishop. 'But he'll only ask you one question. He will look you in the eye and ask, "What do you think of me?".' Christianity, unlike New Age, says the answer to that question has eternal ramifications.

QUeSTiON

1. What would be a good slogan to sum up the underlying beliefs of New Age spirituality?

2. Why is a definition of New Age difficult to pin down?

3. Of each of the forces creating an environment fit for New Age belief (pages 195 to 196), which do you consider the most influential? Why?

DiSCUSSiON

A. How would you account for the rise in interest in New Age belief and practice?

B. How convinced are you by New Age's belief in the essential goodness of humanity?

C. 'The most striking feature of New Age fiction is its unbridled optimism'[30] (Anu Majumdar). What might be the strength and weakness of such a stance?

D. Writer Paul Heelas, says of New Age teaching that it has three elements. 'It explains why life – as conventionally experienced – is not what it should be; it provides an account of what it is to find perfection; and it provides a means for obtaining salvation.'

There are some obvious parallels with Christianity in this assessment. Where do the main differences lie between Christian and New Age teaching?

LOCATING STRENGTH AND HOPE

In his bestselling book, *The Power of Now – a guide to spiritual enlightenment*, Eckart Tolle tells the story of a beggar sitting on the side of the road begging for 30 years. When he asks a stranger for some money the stranger says, 'I have nothing to give you,' but tells him to look inside the box he is sitting on. At first the beggar is reluctant – saying it is just a box and he has sat on it for 30 years. Finally he looks inside and discovers it is full of gold.

Author – Tolle says:

'I am that stranger who has nothing to give you and is telling you to look inside ... inside yourself.

Those who have not found their true wealth, which is the radiant joy of being, and the deep unshakable peace that comes with it, are beggars even if they have great material wealth. They are looking outside for scraps of pleasure or fulfillment, for validation, security, or love, while they have a treasure within that not only includes those things but is infinitely greater than anything the world can offer.'[31]

DiSCUSSiON

E. What is different about this way of understanding reality to the Christian teaching on the nature of humanity and the source of hope?

Do not stand at my grave and weep

I am not there; I do not sleep.

I am a thousand winds that blow,

I am the diamond glints on snow,

I am the sun on ripened grain,

I am the gentle autumn rain.

When you awaken in the morning's hush

I am the swift uplifting rush

Of quiet birds in circling flight.

I am the soft starlight at night.

Do not stand at my grave and cry,

I am not there; I did not die.

MARY E FRYE 1932

DiSCUSSiON

F. Where in the above extract can you locate New Age thinking and belief?

PeRCEPTiON

1. What appear to you to be the most appealing aspects of New Age as a way of viewing the world?

2. What are its most identifiable weaknesses?

INTERVIEW
andrew ireland

Hobbling in on crutches with his right leg in plaster up to his knee Andrew Ireland could be excused for being less cheerful than he is. 'The first and last time I go skateboarding', he smiles.

One gets the impression the accident will be a minor setback for the third-year student of mining engineering. At only 20 years old Andrew appears unusually certain about where he is heading. The career path for mining engineering usually involves 'living in the desert for about five years—probably in Western Australia', he explains. After that, Andrew aims to live and work overseas, 'meeting people, and gaining some different cultural understanding; growing up a bit', he says.

If as *centred* as he appears, Andrew would put this down to a very stable upbringing. 'There was a real sense of security', he explains. The eldest of five kids, raised in a rural coastal setting, Andrew has inherited the Ireland family's love of music. He plays piano, cello, guitar, 'honks on the tuba' and sings in choirs.

An even greater family legacy is a strongly held Christian faith. Andrew sees this as a true gift, but is adamant that ultimately he had to discover it for himself. A quest to find answers involved really doubting whether Christianity was true at all —talking to other Christians and reading books by atheists and 'trying to make myself think', explains Andrew.

His search was not helped by some of the books he read on the reliability of the Bible which Andrew says were not 'even the slightest bit convincing —even to me as a Christian'. He kept reading and finally found some books that began from a basis of asking 'how do we know anything?' or 'how can we know what we know?'. This was a turning point for Andrew and a place from which he could find compelling verification for the teaching from his childhood.

Andrew senses that for young people today the complexity of the modern world and especially the amount of choices open to them means there is 'not a lot of certainty'. In such a context he finds his trust in Jesus offers much solace. 'For me the Christian worldview is a great comfort ... '[It tells me that life is] not unplanned and chaotic—God acted in history and acts in history so he is kind of a part of what goes on, so that's a comforting thing. But I think what makes me get out of bed in the morning is —there is a great hope—it is amazing to be this [otherwise] insignificant person walking around and [knowing] the creator of the universe cares for you and says in the future when you die I want you to come and live with me.'

When asked to consider the pervasive messages of our culture, Andrew has little hesitation, 'The message you get from music and media is "nobody really knows what we are supposed to be doing—but everyone likes to have fun and enjoy themselves, so pleasure is your highest goal".'

Interestingly, Andrew says the academic world effectively has only a slightly different message when it comes to the bigger questions of life. 'The message seems to be "we have thought a lot about meaning and purpose—there has been a lot of confusion and therefore we don't really know ... so as long as *you* are satisfied and have a sense of achievement in your life you have done well",' he suggests.

His observation of the dominant thought in the arts faculty is that it is all about having a discussion. 'It's not whether you can convince me or I can convince you, it's about the journey, and the debate is the final task rather than reaching a final answer. I reckon almost no-one I know has been satisfied with that', says Andrew.

Andrew's observations suggest that the modernist framework is far from redundant when it comes to thinking about spiritual issues. 'Perhaps the fact that we have discovered so much *truth*—in terms of scientific truth—we have discovered things about the world which really *are*—and we have built things that rely on these truths—we have buildings and aeroplanes and structures, and we know a lot about the human body and we can fix it—there is progress and things that *are* true about the world, so matters like 'how do we know what happens after death? ... [well] there is a reluctance to talk about things you can't nail down and prove', he says.

When attention turns to the nature of humanity, Andrew says humans have been created by God and are made 'in his image'. Right and wrong he senses, emerge from both an instinctive response (implying a natural law) and from the worldview that we all hold. 'Your picture of how things fit together and where God sits, or doesn't sit, then allows you to make decisions about right and wrong', he says.

Accordingly, the chief purpose for us as human beings is to 'love God and those around us,' says Andrew. 'I think if we have been created by God then our primary responsibility is to him.'

4000087

CHAPTER 10

I buy, therefore I am

CONSUMERISM

Geoff Broughton

> Inner liberty depends upon being exempt from domination of things as well as from domination of people. There are many who have acquired a high degree of political and social liberty, but only very few are not enslaved to things.
>
> ABRAHAM JOSHUA HESCHEL[1]

INTRODUCTION

I was recently confronted by a disturbing image in *Adbusters* magazine. The image was of a distended brown belly beside a picture of a bloated white belly. The caption below was even more disturbing: 'one billion people are dying of starvation. Another billion are dying of excess.' Merely being able to read this book automatically places you in the second category. We live in that part of the world where people generally have 'too much' rather than 'not enough'. We are living in a period of time some are calling 'The Age of the Consumer', where we find our identity and meaning in life through acquisition and accumulation: 'I buy (shop), therefore I am.'

Australian Institute director Clive Hamilton provocatively called this 'affluenza' in his 2004 book of the same name.[2] Yet most Australians (and probably the vast majority of those living in the First World) don't consider themselves sick with greed. In Australia, we pride ourselves on being a land where everyone gets a 'fair go'. But if we define greed as taking more than our fair share, then the evidence is against us. In 1998 the United Nations Development Program estimated a child born in Australia would consume the same as 30–50 children born in developing countries. Our appetites have grown since that estimate was made, and we are consuming even more. When Sydney hosted the 2000 Olympic Games, monthly retail sales were less than $13 billion. By 2004 they were almost $17 billion. With inflation low and population growth modest, one wonders what has changed in four years to require $4 billion more spending each month?

Consumption of such magnitude has become a way of life and does not have a neatly organised system of ideas or beliefs. There are no great thinkers who are the key 'proponents' of consumerism. Nearly everyone is a consumer. There are those who have more because they consume more, just as there are those who have less because they consume less. Very few people choose to opt out of consumer culture by 'not consuming'. Economics is one way of exploring how consumption has become such an unavoidable part of living in the twenty-first century.

We find ourselves in a culture that defines our relationships and actions primarily through a matrix of consumption. As the philosopher Baudrillard explains, "Consumption is a system of meaning". We assign value to ourselves and others based on the goods we purchase. One's identity is now constructed by the clothes you wear, the vehicle you drive, and the music on your iPod.

SKYE JETHANI

HISTORY

Only a few generations ago, people produced (mainly food and other essentials) for their own use. This is what economists call subsistence production. The market had its origins as a place where farmers (and others) could sell their excess produce. Today, people produce an endless array of goods and services that will be consumed almost exclusively by others. The 'market' has evolved and grown from being local and mainly agricultural, to being global and all-pervasive. It is the extension of the market into every sphere of life that forces us to become consumers. Our daily food is bought at the 'super' market. The ever-expanding growth of the market has brought massive changes to our lives that are largely invisible to us. For example, we once worked in order to survive, and provide for our loved ones, as perhaps our great-grandparents did. Today we work to make money and buy a lifestyle. Increasingly this lifestyle is defined by possessing certain 'luxury' items—the latest mobile phone or iPod, and their many accessories.

Commodification[5] refers to the process by which goods and services once provided through self-provision become commodities to be bought and sold in the marketplace. For example, once you might have made your child's birthday cake, thrown a child's birthday party at home, done your own cleaning and ironing, washed your own car or made your own custard. But now, you could opt to buy a birthday cake, pay a local centre to run your child's birthday party, employ a cleaner or someone to do the ironing, pay to have someone wash the car and buy custard from the supermarket. When goods or services are exchanged in the marketplace economists call them commodities. Older generations can remember when many daily items like clothing, furniture and tools were made at home rather than bought at a shop. Recently I discovered that my grandfather made the bricks to

Our enormously productive economy ...demands that we make consumption our way of life, that we convert the buying and use of goods into rituals, that we seek our spiritual satisfaction, our ego satisfaction, in consumption ...We need things consumed, burned up, worn out, replaced, and discarded at an ever-increasing rate.

VICTOR LEBOW (RETAILING ANALYST 1955)[4]

build a garage when he purchased his first car. Each evening after work, he would mix up a batch of sand and cement, fashion some new bricks, so that on the weekend he would have a couple of dozen new bricks to lay! I'm about as likely to make my own bricks as I am to make my own car! When I choose to make something (as opposed to purchasing it at a shop) it is either a cup of coffee or a sandwich. And in any given week, I buy more coffees at the cafe than I brew at home.

Consequently commodification affects almost every area of life. This has fundamentally changed the way contemporary societies are organised, how we relate as neighbours, friends and even family, as well as the way we relate to our governments, schools, universities and voluntary groups like clubs, churches and sporting teams.

As our lives become dominated by the marketplace and what economists call 'exchange relations' our identity increasingly becomes that of a consumer. We become part of the system informed and formed by the values of the marketplace. The central idea of markets is individualism. The market assumes that individuals know best what they want and that by engaging in the marketplace they are free to express their desires and needs— economists call this 'utility maximisation'.

The New York Times has estimated that the average American is exposed to 3,500 ads per day.[6]

MATERIAL SATISFACTION?

'Many studies show that materialism – the pursuit of money and possessions – seems to breed not happiness but dissatisfaction, depression, anxiety, anger, isolation, and alienation. People for whom "extrinsic goals" such as fame, fortune and glamour are a priority in life tend to experience more anxiety and depression and lower overall wellbeing – and to be less trusting and caring in their relationships – than people oriented towards "intrinsic goals" of close relationships, personal growth and self-understanding, and contributing to the community. In short, the more materialistic people are, the poorer their quality of life.'

ECKERSLEY, WIERENGA AND WYN[7]

CENTRAL BELIEFS

The pursuit of economic growth is the engine room of individual, corporate, national and global consuming. While most people saw the irony of the 1980s mantra 'greed is good', the idea that 'growth is good' remains a fundamental economic principle. Many of us will remember the pictures in our high school economic textbooks of an African or Asian farmer who was able to produce enough only for his or her family. This was described as 'subsistence' living—not being able to produce enough to sell on the market.

Economists would argue (and who could disagree?) that growth would be a good thing for this farmer, his family, village and nation. In the same way, the growing business of backyard or home office entrepreneurs into their first factory or shopfront should be celebrated.

If a fundamental principle of economics is 'growth is good' then another follows—that 'the market is god'. The twentieth century triumph of capitalism over communism—the free market over centralised control—emphasises the point.

Some economists will defend the excessive salaries of CEOs, or the ridiculous advertising contracts of sports stars, simply because they are determined by 'market forces'.

But this also raises the tricky issue of distribution. The benefits of ever-expanding economic growth are not shared equally. While there is no shortage of advertising endorsements for the successful sports star, the subsistence farmer may have trouble getting a fair price for his rice or coffee at the markets. Awareness-raising campaigns such as 'free trade versus fair trade' highlight the problem of market forces being the sole determinant in distribution.

The commercial reaches out to sell more than a service or product; it sells a way of understanding the world.

STUART AND ELIZABETH EWEN [8]

Another key principle undergirding modern economics is that *supply is scarce.* The idea of scarcity cries out 'there is not enough'. Contemporary consumer culture operates on the central tenet that there is not enough to go around. 'You'll miss out' is an idea that feeds our anxieties and insecurities that branding and corporate advertising relies on. Old Testament scholar Walter Brueggemann says:

> The myth of scarcity makes us each an agent of acquisitiveness in the face of all the others who also pursue acquisitiveness.[9]

The almighty power of the market can also surprise those who have gained most from it. We are becoming more aware that unbridled economic growth has social and ecological costs. In the twenty-first century, many large corporations are attempting to reflect these concerns by addressing a 'triple bottom line'—monetary profits, together with environmental sustainability and social responsibility. The market brings about these shifts as consumers buy from what they regard as fair and responsible companies.

Some remain suspicious of these developments, and whether 'triple bottom line' reporting is all it is cracked up to be. Actual sales figures of these environmentally friendly and socially responsible products show there is still a long way to go.[10]

Although economics and theology are vastly different disciplines,[11] a few initial observations are worth making from a Christian perspective (which I will develop later). Obviously economic theory does not actually teach that 'the market' is any kind of divine entity. Those who believe that any rival to God is a form of idolatry must challenge the market's god-like function. Jesus said that we cannot serve two masters. Both God and the market cannot be sovereign. The philosophy of 'growth-at-all-costs' is directly opposed by the 'jubilee economics' practised by God's people throughout the Old Testament.

Widows and strangers were allowed to pick up the leftovers from the corner of fields being harvested and interest *wasn't* charged on loans. But perhaps most radical of all, property returned to the original owners every fifty years (the jubilee year), ensuring a kind of generational justice, where current generations were not permitted to steal from future generations. This kind of jubilee economics was grounded in the character of a generous God, for whom the key principle is abundance, not scarcity.

IMPACT

I denied myself nothing my eyes desired;

I refused my heart no pleasure.

My heart took delight in all my work,and this was the reward for all my labour.

Yet when I surveyed all that my hands had done and what I had toiled to achieve,

everything was meaningless, a chasing after the wind; nothing was gained under the sun.

ECCLESIASTES 2:10–11

It would be impossible to overstate the impact consumerism has had on the Western world. It is so much part of life that few of us pause to question the underlying assumptions that drive the urge to consume.

One of the implications of individualism as expressed in the market is that individuals become the primary unit of analysis and the focus of all activity. This means that advertisers direct all their attention to the individual, to you and me – not our community, our environment or our city. As part of this message we are told that acquisition will bring some sort of satisfaction—the marketplace becomes our treasure trove—a font of endless possibilities where our many desires and dreams might one day be made a reality. It is an attractive and seductive message.

Advertising itself has undergone something of a revolution in response to the increasingly central role of the consumer. At the turn of the millennium, Naomi Klein identified the trend away from advertising products to developing brand identities.[12] For example, the BMW has been cleverly marketed as the 'best car in the world', even though the vast majority of people would know very little about the quality of a BMW compared with an Audi or a Lexus. This is because branding focuses our attention away from the 'product' to the 'personality', which can be understood as a lifestyle, an image, an identity or even a set of values. The CEO of Gucci says it succinctly:

> [Luxury] brands are more than goods. The goods are secondary because first of all you buy into a brand, then you buy the products. They give people the opportunity to live a dream.[13]

Attempts to resist the effect of corporate advertising and branding are made difficult by another dimension of consumer culture: its ability to quickly *commodify* alternatives, which are incorporated into the mainstream. The world of fashion and music illustrate how this happens.

If you were born after the mid 1960s, you cannot remember the time when jeans were considered a radical (working class) alternative to traditional pants. By the late 1960s everybody and anybody wore jeans. In our lifetime we have seen a number of changes to the pair of jeans that began life as some kind of sub-cultural protest, but were quickly *commodified* and incorporated into the mainstream. First, during the 1980s the ripped appearance of an old, worn out pair of jeans was deemed fashionable. Very quickly a range of pre-washed, stonewashed, faded and factory-ripped jeans could be purchased right off the shelf. By 2006 this fashion trend had spread to most clothes: faded, distressed polo shirts, faded, distressed jeans, faded, distressed cargo pants and shorts, faded and distressed leather sandals and striped shirts. The 'pre-owned' look was mainstream. Similarly, during the 1990s, the alternative trend of wearing baggy jeans lower on the hips, rather than skin-tight jeans around the waist, became the latest innovation quickly incorporated into their design.

SUBSTANCE OR STYLE?

'Style ... is a way of saying who we are or, perhaps more correctly, who we want to be perceived as being. Our consumer paradise offers us a rich palette from which to paint this image of ourselves consisting of stylised goods, name brands, logos, fashions, new looks, retro looks, reshaped noses and breasts, whitened teeth and exotic accessories which are all delivering information ... style is how we stand out, how we say who we are, how we assert our unique individuality. So from these purchases we assemble the parts of who we want to be, the parts which can combine in different ways as the whole comes together each day ... Of course! God has done a disappearing act and what are we left with? Only what is shifting and changing, what is superficial and impermanent, only with ourselves and what we can make of ourselves.'

DAVID F. WELLS[14]

In today's consumer culture, 'new' music cannot remain alternative for very long. The rebellious roots of rock, punk, and grunge, plus a host of others, have been *commodified* and made mainstream. At the turn of the millennium, artists began posting their latest recordings directly on the internet, as a protest against the corporate power of the recording studios. MP 3s have made online music mainstream (and big business!).

Even traditional religions like Christianity have been affected (some would argue seduced) by consumerism. In a recent book called *Selling Spirituality,* the authors argue that the replacement of tradition-specific religion with a more free-form search for personal meaning has resulted in a consumerist spirituality that promises the world but demands absolutely nothing:

> In a sense, the most troubling aspect of many modern spiritualities is precisely that they are not troubling enough.[15]

These flourishing expressions of consumer spirituality (what the authors call *capitalist spirituality*) ultimately serve the profit margins rather than faithful devotion. Increasingly those attending church (or mosque, synagogue or temple) are treated as consumers of a spiritual brand or product.

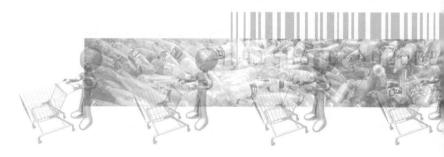

The consumer is schooled in insatiability. He or she is never to be satisfied – at least, not for long. The consumer is tutored that people basically consist of unmet needs that can be appeased by commodified goods and experiences. Accordingly, the consumer should think first and foremost of himself or herself and meeting his or her felt needs. The consumer is taught to value above all else freedom, freedom defined as a vast array of choices.[16]

RODNEY CLAPP

As noted earlier, some see the process of commodification as a simple (and neutral) outworking of market forces. Others are more enthusiastic, seeing the market's ability to both correct its own excesses and to constantly re-invent itself.

In accepting there is some truth in both observations, I refuse to believe that commodification is a wholly positive, or even neutral development.

Along with contemporary figures such as Jeffrey Sachs (Harvard Professor of Economics)[17], Bono of U2 (activist/celebrity of popular culture)[18], and Vandana Shiva (an environmental guru from India)[19], I believe those of us with too much need to focus more attention on those with not enough. And there is enough evidence to suggest that we are not alone.

Recently, Australians have shown greater willingness to 'dig deep' when a national or international crisis grabs our attention, as with the tsunami of 26 December 2004. Private donations to Australian aid agencies have increased by an average of 9.5 percent per year since 2000. In the case of some Christian aid and development agencies, the increase is even greater. Conversely, people like Vandana Shiva are critical of the way westerners think that by throwing money at these problems they will somehow get better instead of worse.

Lasting solutions may indeed be elusive. Who has the answers? Who should we believe? Theorists of globalisation and global culture have often noted that the world now resembles a large shopping arcade or supermarket.[20] So it seems with the choices regarding our world's future.

Positively, the current generation of young people have been raised with a greater awareness of global issues through *CNN* and the web, and seem more inclined to be concerned about issues of economic justice such as debt relief for African nations, and the difference between fair trade and free trade. More young Australians are choosing to live and work overseas, some for multinational corporations, others with groups focussed on global issues like the World Trade Organisation, the World Bank, and the International Monetary Fund. Time will tell whether campaigns like 'Make Poverty History' and the Millennium Development Goals succeed in bringing any lasting change. But globalisation has raised awareness of the effects of our 'conspicuous consumption' on everyone else.

Simultaneously, more individuals and families are living in Australia with unsustainable levels of expectation and debt.

Research suggests the current generation of young people leaving school will find it harder to afford an education, get a job, or buy a home and they will have a huge group of aging baby-boomers to support in their retirement.

We now know that we are facing an energy crisis (when the world's consumption of fossil fuel will exceed the future reserves) and an ecological crisis (climate change). As suggested earlier, both are closely connected to our current levels of consumption.

CONTINENTAL DRIFT

Writing in 1932, Spanish philosopher Jose Ortega y Gasset spoke of the nature of modern technological society as a 'mass' society in which cultural and political aspirations are surrendered to the lowest common denominator of comfort, convenience and safety. He said we live in a time:

'when man believes himself fabulously capable of creation, but he does not know what to create. Lord of all things, he is not lord of himself. He feels lost amid his own abundance. With more means at its disposal, more knowledge, more technique than ever, it turns out that the world today goes the same way as the worst of worlds that have been; it simply drifts.'[22]

CONTACT AND DEPARTURE FROM CHRISTIANITY

Christianity (along with most other spiritual traditions) contends that people are relational beings, and ultimate fulfilment or satisfaction is not achieved individually. Although Christians believe in a *personal* God, this God is revealed to be relational. The very character of God is found in relationships between Father, Son and Spirit. In creating, sustaining and reconciling the world and humanity, God is deeply relational.

Surprising for some, is the growing consensus of economists that our excessive consumption is not achieving what we think it might: greater happiness. Anyone who has spent even a moment in self-reflection knows this already. But we continue to consume more, not less. Last year I purchased a second-hand sea-kayak, a sport I had not been involved in since my late teens. Twelve months later, I have purchased another kayak from a paddling mate who happened to be selling his, which was better than mine. I am also equipped with four new life-jackets (for my wife and two kids), a new paddle, a headlamp for paddling at night, a hand pump, a dry bag for car keys and mobile phone, and I look longingly at a whole range of gadgets and clothing in a magazine I now buy called *Sea-kayak*. I still love my new toy, and I try to get out on the water once or twice a week—but since the initial purchase I have consumed more, not less.

As a Christian, I am troubled by my high consumption, and of those around me. Together we have been seduced into thinking we will never have enough. Ultimately, I find myself *consumed* by this way of life. The never-ending pursuit of acquisitions, the luxurious lifestyle that remains tantalisingly just out of reach, the burden of growing debt, the pace of life that wants to grab each and every opportunity ... together become all-consuming.

In sharp contrast to this idea of scarcity, the God of the Bible is about abundance. From the first chapters of the Genesis story, we see an abundant God at work:

- God initiates abundance—calling forth plants and fish and birds and animals.

- God promises continued abundance—commanding all these to 'increase and multiply'.

- God is satisfied with creation's abundance, declaring it all 'very good'.

- God rests: having set in motion a world of abundance the world will have enough.

Although some forms of Christianity are aggressively against materialism, the biblical account affirms the essential *goodness* of what God created. For those with the eyes to see, creation is not just 'there'—it's given by God.

As the apostle Paul wrote at the end of one of his letters:

> "Who has ever given to God, that God should repay him?
> For from him and through him and to him are all things."

ROMANS 11:35-36

God the creator is a generous gift-giver, and God intended that people receive and enjoy his gifts.

Enron – the smartest guys in the room

This 2005 documentary charts the way Enron collapsed from being the seventh largest company in the US with assets of around 100 billion dollars, to being bankrupt within a year. In the scandal, investors and employees were left with nothing, while executives walked away with billions. Commenting on the incident, Charles Colson asks whether 'modern secularism has undermined the foundation essential for democratic capitalism.' He highlights Michael Novak's argument likening Western liberal democracy to a three-legged stool, comprising political freedom, economic freedom and moral responsibility. The collapse of Enron is emblematic of a rotten third leg, says Colson. '[The Bible] balances acquisition of wealth with a demand for both justice and compassion, and requires people to subordinate self-interest to moral demands'.[23] The problem is, without a basis on which to decide what moral demands we should follow, a consumerist culture awash in secularism has nothing substantial to attach itself to.

Yet the rest of the Bible tells the story of human distrust of divine abundance. From the beginning people were dissatisfied. God's creatures wanted more. And so the Genesis story continues as the bountiful earth becomes stingy—daily food now requires sweat and tears. Scarcity sets in and paradise is lost. The history of the Hebrew people is a history of learning to trust God's abundance. So central was this issue to the Hebrew people they had a special name for it: *Dayenu*—the attitude that says:

> 'there is enough', more than enough, because 'there is enough in God's goodness'.[24]

If the God of the Bible really is a God of abundance, how might this shape attitudes and behaviour when it comes to consuming? The role of wealth and acquiring possessions in Christian thought is quite diverse. Sharp differences in attitude and lifestyles can be traced to the tensions that arise in Christian thought and teaching. A brief survey of the main themes that arise through the narrative of the Bible illustrates these tensions.[25]

In Hebrew or early Jewish thought, what Christians call the Old Testament, we begin with the goodness of wealth because it is the blessing of God. God blesses certain people such as Abraham who, in turn, should become a blessing to others. Certain restrictions are also found in those Old Testament books known as 'The Law', governing the accumulation of wealth, particularly property. Everything belongs to God, and God wants all to enjoy it. By the time the Hebrew people had developed into a nation-state, with their own king, gaps had emerged between those with too much and those with too little. Wealth and property increasingly belonged to a few. The 'prophets' spoke powerfully against this lack of economic justice. The 'sins' of the people of God were closely linked with selfish attitudes towards wealth, evidenced by a lack of care of those in need. The more poetic writings, called 'Wisdom literature', describe the tension around possessions and accumulating wealth. On the one hand possessions can be a reward for faithfulness and hard work. On the other, there are repeated warnings against the rich, often called 'the wicked', who accumulated their wealth dishonestly, or at the expense of others.

With the development of specifically Christian thought in the New Testament, there is one *significant* difference: wealth and possessions are never promised as a reward for faithfulness or obedience. The nuances of the wisdom literature give way to the more radical teaching and lifestyle of Jesus Christ. God and money are rival masters, and Jesus repeatedly asked his listeners to choose God. Jesus and his band of disciples voluntarily lived with limited incomes. They accumulated few possessions for the sake of God's kingdom, relying on the generosity and hospitality of others. Likewise the early Christians pooled their resources and possessions, and lived generously with each other and outsiders. By the end of the New Testament writings, there are strong warnings against the emerging divisions between wealthy and poor people (see the letter of James) and against forgetting generosity (see Paul's two letters to the Corinthians).

Very importantly the New Testament challenges us to ask where we place our trust. Jesus' parable of the rich fool (Luke 12:13–21) urges people to be 'rich before God' rather than relying on physical wealth in the present. While we can enjoy the good things of life now, relationship with God and each other is a priority according to biblical teaching.

If Hebrew thought celebrated *dayenu* (there is enough in God's goodness), then Christian thought celebrates grace (the goodness of God in the person of Jesus Christ). Both are expressions of the generosity of God. Consequently contemporary Christian thought generally remains suspicious about accumulating wealth, greed and acquisitiveness and ever-increasing consumption.[26]

God's generosity, and God's abundance offers the possibility of living more simply (acquiring less) and more generously. Simple, generous lifestyles shaped by generous communities are a powerful challenge to the pervasive culture of consumerism.

RESPONSE

QUeST¿ON

1. What would be a good slogan to sum up the underlying beliefs of Consumerism?

2. Do you agree that consumerism is in fact a problem?

3. What are the costs to society of rampant consumerism?

4. What might be some potential benefits of reducing consumption in your own life? Try to think of some specific ways your life could change if you were to resist consumerism.

DiSCUSS¿ON

A. 'My view of the world is that everybody is medicated on something: plastic surgery, drugs, sex, religion, shopping ... We're a culture that anaesthetises ourselves with things. And we're also a culture that really tries hard to find meaning where sometimes there isn't any meaning.'

   RYAN MURPHY (CREATOR OF TV DRAMA NIP/TUCK)

   How much do you think consumerism is a part of this 'anesthetising' element of our culture?

B. One criticism of some modern economic policy and practice is that people as well as things are regarded as commodities, and that the market determines a person's worth.

   Do you agree that this is the case? In what way is such practice in conflict with a Christian view of the world?

ESCAPING THE TRAP

In the US a group of about fifty teachers, engineers, executives and other professionals have formed what they call the Compact, pledging not to buy anything new other than food, medicine and other essentials. They aim to buy only used goods and rely on second-hand stores, flea markets and eBay to do so. Happiness through simplicity is the aim.[27]

Mike Hanley, in the Australian Financial Review says, 'The failure of a consumer society to deliver high levels of personal happiness has become a perplexing question of great interest, not just to economists, but to society as a whole. It's known as the happiness paradox'.[28]

The Compact is an attempt to answer this paradox. John Perry, a member of Compact says, 'We're trying to get off the first-market consumerism grid, because consumer culture is destroying the world'.[29] Their concerns centre on environmental and social damage created by consumerist culture. The only way to stop it is to get off the merry-go-round they say.

High school teacher Kate Boyd says the initiative gives her more time, money, and a healthier perspective on life. 'It's just a relief to get away from the pressure to always have new clothes, gadgets and other things we don't need,' she said.

Some commentators suggest the Compact is part of a larger trend away from the all-pervasive consumerism. Time will tell, if they are right.

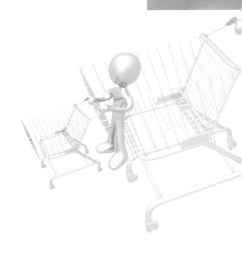

DiSCUSSiON

C. How do you account for the phenomenon described in the article?

D. What do you think brings lasting satisfaction in life?

PeRCEPTiON

1. What are the most appealing aspects of consumerism as a way of viewing the world?

2. What are its most identifiable weaknesses?

looking ahead

Matt stopped for a rest halfway through packing up his room. Outside the warmth of the day and the smell of freshly cut grass offered up the promise of summer holidays and opportunity. The panic of recent days cramming at 3am for exams was over. Matt thought he'd probably make it through to next year. He was getting the hang of this student thing.

The debris that surrounded Matt provided a snapshot of the year gone by. In the corner was the American Indian headdress, now looking especially tired, that he'd worn to the fancy dress ball in July. There were 'borrowed' number plates, ripped wall posters, and the minor-premiers trophy for Rugby. A mock certificate from the pub-crawl; both a badge of honour and source of private shame. In a drawer he discovered a crumpled pass to the north coast blues festival he and three others had hitchhiked to at Easter, a block of surf wax, and an old card from Suzie, offering a final consoling goodbye. He smiled at this, remembering his initial shock and overly dramatic reaction to the break up. After a couple of nights staring at the ceiling, he had managed to recover fairly quickly.

Buried deep in the drawer was a funeral service-sheet Matt couldn't bring himself to throw away. Life had returned to normal after the accident and the smudged photographs of the two guys stared back at him in silent protest that they be forgotten so quickly. Matt hadn't known either of them well. They had been in the year ahead of him, and the taller one, Jed, had played in his rugby team. He wasn't even sure he liked them much, and for that he felt a strange sense of guilt. He had a memory of absolute clarity of the night they were killed. There was a big party at the college and the whole place was bursting with energy and life. It was like a frozen moment, like musical statues when he was

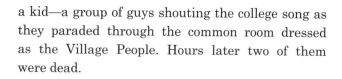

a kid—a group of guys shouting the college song as they paraded through the common room dressed as the Village People. Hours later two of them were dead.

The funeral had been surreal. His enduring memory was the mother of one of the boys sobbing hysterically beside the coffin, her husband looking on, confused, helpless and heartbroken. Matt had never experienced the intrusion of death before. He had a picture in his mind of their bodies cold and rotting in the ground. Whenever the image came to him it felt like poison.

Matt found himself wondering about his own life and its purpose, and some of the big questions. What was God like? If he even existed. What's the point of all the things we spend our time striving for? Are we alone in the universe? Where do we find hope? It seemed to Matt that plenty of others were seeking answers in their own way and at uni there was no shortage of places to go on that search. But whom should you believe? Matt had even gone to church a couple of times with his Christian friend Tom. He liked Tom and admired his commitment to his faith. He was a normal guy and didn't try to shove his beliefs down your throat. Matt envied Tom's quiet assurance. There was something appealing about what Tom was into and it nagged at Matt for a while, although he managed to push it to the back of his mind.

He found himself gaining confidence at university and more able to 'mix it' in this world of ideas. In a sociology tutorial Matt surprised himself by getting into a debate with his Marxist professor and more or less holding his own. His attitude to these academic giants—the gods of the university —was not what it once was. Seeing his psychology professor Dr Landers, breeze through the foyer of an inner city cinema wearing a Kaftan and bare feet, was something of a turning point for Matt. Somehow from that moment on these towering figures of

wisdom and knowledge appeared more human and less intimidating.

'I guess we all have to find our own compass in life', offered Francesca as she slurped some kind of iced fruit concoction with an odd green hue. Matt couldn't imagine what might be in it. 'But surely it's no good if the compass leads you nowhere', Matt responded. This brought only a shrug and more slurping. Matt had been in a couple of classes with Francesca, and they had started meeting at the cafeteria in between lectures. She was so different to him, but he had to admit he was starting to really like her. They argued a lot, but it was more sparring and debate than anything else and Matt was beginning to wonder if the attraction might be mutual.

He knew he wouldn't see her over summer and was starting to feel bummed about that. None of his mates knew about her yet, but Matt sensed he would miss her. They didn't have much in common, but what they did share was a desire for answers and they both had minds that were increasingly hungry. Francesca might be more comfortable with ambiguity than Matt, but he knew she wasn't satisfied with what she'd found so far.

'If someone wants to offer me a compass I want to know where it's going to take me', Matt said by way of closing the discussion. That too he knew to be a false hope as Francesca always got the last word.

When she left three days ago, they'd exchanged an awkward goodbye—a back patting hug during which Matt lingered too long. It seemed he could never be truly cool. Anyway, now there was packing to be done. A summer job, parties, and trips up the coast awaited. Matt felt good about what lay ahead. The pulsing energy of youth surged inside him. He felt like he was beginning to understand who he was, and maybe, just maybe, the answers to some big questions may lie around the next corner. SS

endnotes

INTRODUCTION—LIFE VISIONS

1. James H. Olthuis, 'On worldviews,' in *Stained Glass – Worldviews and social science* (University Press of America, London UK, 1989), pg 29.

2. David K. Naugle, *Worldview – The history of a concept* (Eerdmans Grand Rapids Michigan, 2002), pg 298.

3. In the following categories I am following the work of Julie Mitchell in *Teaching about Worldviews and Values,* (The Council for Christian Education in Schools, Melbourne Australia, 2004), pg 8 and James Sire, *Naming the Elephant– worldview as a concept,* (IVP Downers Grove, Illinois, 2004), pg 2.

4. James Sire, *Naming the Elephant – Worldview as a concept,* (IVP Downers Grove, Illinois, 2004), pg 96.

5. Olthuis, pg 29.

6. Ibid., pg 29.

7. Sire, pg 101.

8. Naugle, pgs 302–3.

9. Mitchell, pg 10.

10. Olthuis, pg 33.

11. Sire, pg 106.

12. Naugle, pg 327.

13. Ibid.

14. Ibid., pg 328.

15. James Sire, *Naming the Elephant – Worldview as a concept,* (IVP Downers Grove, Illinois, 2004), pg 115.

16. Naugle, pgs 296–297.

CHAPTER 1—CHRISTIANITY

1. 80.1% and 5.3% respectively. Source: *World Values Survey,* Inter-university Consortium for Political and Social Research (Ronald Inglehart et al. 2000).

2. A starting point for investigating the historical basis of Christianity can be found in the author's *The Christ Files: How Historians Know What they Know about Jesus* (Blue Bottle Books, 2005).

3. Josephus, *Jewish Antiquities* 18.63.

4. An accessible introduction to the historical data concerning Jesus' reported miracles, along with an explanation of their meaning according to the Christian Gospels, can be found in the author's *A Spectator's Guide to Jesus: An introduction to the man from Nazareth* (Blue Bottle Books, 2005, pp 35–48). Representative of the mainstream scholarly conclusion that Jesus performed deeds which friend and foe alike took to be miraculous is the 500 pg discussion by prolific US scholar, John P Meier, *A Marginal Jew: Rethinking the historical Jesus,* vol. 2 (Doubleday, 1994, pp 507–1038).

5. The account of the Roman trial of Jesus can be found in John 18: 33–37.

6. Representative of this mainstream scholarly conclusion about the resurrection traditions are Professor James Dunn of the University of Durham (*Jesus Remembered.* Eerdmans, 2003, pp.825–79) and Professor Graham Stanton of Cambridge University (*The Gospels and Jesus.* Oxford: Oxford University Press, 2002, pp.269–299).

7. C. S. Lewis, *Mere Christianity* (HarperCollins, 1997), pg 43.

8. At the end of a lengthy explanation of Jesus' resurrection and lordship we find the following encouragement to approach life with fresh resolve: 'Therefore, my dear brothers, stand firm. Let nothing move you. Always give yourselves fully to the work of the Lord, because you know that your labour in the Lord is not in vain' (1 Corinthians 15:58).

9. The Lord's Prayer, as it is called, can be found in Matthew 6:9–13.

CHAPTER 2—MODERNISM

1. Peter L. Berger, quoted in Craig M. Gay, *The way of the (modern world) – or why it's tempting to live as if God doesn't exist* (Eerdmans Publishing, Grand Rapids Michigan, Paternoster Press Carlisle, Cumbria, Regent College Publishing, Vancouver, 1998), pg 10.

2. A good reader on the topic is Lawrence Cahoone(ed.), From *Modernism to Postmodernism: An Anthology* (Blackwell Philosophy Anthologies, Blackwell Publishers, Oxford, 2002).

3. For a good summary book, see Steven Shapin, *The scientific revolution* (The University of Chicago Press, Chicago and London, 1996).

4. Francis Bacon, *The Advancement of Learning and New Atlantis* (Oxford University Press, London, 1960).

5. See Thomas Sprat, *History of the Royal Society* (1667), paperback edition (Kessinger Publishing Co, Montana, 2003).

6. Descartes' works are available in Penguin Classics.

7. For a good summary, see Norman Hampson, *The Enlightenment* (Penguin Books, Harmondsworth, 1990).

8. For a modern edition see Thomas Paine, *The age of reason*, edited by Moncure Daniel (Dover Publications, NY, 2004).

9. Professor Roy E. Peacock in *Real Science Real Faith* (Monarch Crowborough, 1991), pg 32.

10. Rodney Stark, *For the Glory of God: How monotheism led to reformations, witch-hunts, and the end of slavery* (Princeton University Press, 2004).

11. Stark is not the first to put forward such a theory. Writing in 1926 Alfred N. Whitehead said that science required 'the inexpungable belief that every detailed occurrence can be correlated with its antecedents in a perfectly divine manner, exemplifying general [rational] principles ... It is this instinctive conviction, vividly poised before the imagination, which is the motive power of research; that there is a secret, a secret to be unveiled ...' (Quoted in Craig M Gay, *The Way of the (modern) world, or why it is tempting to live as if God doesn't exist* (Eerdmans Publishing, Grand Rapids Michigan, Paternoster Press Carlisle, Cumbria, Regent College Publishing, Vancouver, 1998), pg 108.

12. There are many good books on this kind of historical interaction between religion and science. Two that deal with the Enlightenment era are David C. Lindberg and Ronal L. Numbers, *God and nature: historical essays on the encounter between Christianity*

and science (University of California Press, Berkeley and others, 1986); and John Hedley Brooke, Science and religion: Some historical perspectives (Cambridge University Press, Cambridge, 1991).

13. See David Hume, *Dialogues Concerning Natural Religion, and the Natural History of Religion* (Oxford Paperbacks, Oxford, 1998).

14. For interest in the reliability of scripture see F.F. Bruce, *New Testament History* (Doubleday, 1969); J Dickson, *The Christ Files – How historians know what they know about Jesus* (Blue Bottle Books, 2006); P Barnett, *Is the New Testament History?* (revised, Aquila Press, 2003).

15. Gay, pg 10.

16. Most of these points come from Greg Clarke's chapter on postmodernism on pg 59 of this book.

17. Gay, pg 11.

18. Edward Friedkin quoted in James Sire, *The Universe next door – A basic worldview catalogue 4th edition* (Intervarsity Press, UK), pg 57.

19. Carl Sagan quoted in Sire, pg 61.

20. Francis Schaeffer, 'The God who is there,' in *The complete works of Francis Schaeffer, Vol 1,* (Crossway books, Wheaton, Illinois, 1982) pg 124.

21. David F. Wells, *Above all earthly pow'rs – Christ in a Postmodern World* (Eerdmans Publishing, Grand Rapids Michigan, 2005), pg 31.

22. Neil Postman, 'Science and the Story we need' © *First Things* 69 (Jan '97) pgs 29–32.

CHAPTER 3—POSTMODERNISM

1. Gene Edward Veith, Jnr., *Postmodern Times – A Christian Guide to Contemporary Thought and Culture* (Crossway Books, Wheaton Illinois, 1994), pg 83.

2. John G. Stackhouse Jnr., *Humble Apologetics – defending the faith today* (Oxford University Press, New York, New York, 2002), pg 26.

3. Ibid., pg 27.

4. Tom Wolfe, *I am Charlotte Simmons* (Jonathan Cape Random House London, UK, 2004), pg 393.

5. Stackhouse., pg 26.

6. Veith, pg 125.

7. Veith, pg 82.

CHAPTER 4—UTILITARIANISM

1. www.paradise-engineering.com/quotation (accessed 12/12/06)

2. J.J.C. Smart and Bernard Williams, *Utilitarianism: For and against* (Cambridge: Cambridge University Press, 1973). The scenarios are by Williams, pgs 97–99.

3. For an older but still useful summary, see Ian C.M. Fairweather and James I.H. McDonald, *The Quest for Christian Ethics* (Edinburgh: Handsel, 1984), pgs 44–55.

4. Smart, in Smart and Williams, pg 49.

5. For useful summaries, see Tim Chappell, 'Utilitarianism', in *Routledge Encyclopedia of Philosophy*, ed. Edward Craig (London: Routledge, 1998) and

Ron Roizen, 'God and the English Utilitarians', (Unpublished graduate student paper, Sociology Department, University of California, Berkeley, 1983); online: http://www.roizen.com/ron/bentham.htm (accessed 12/07/2006). Some of the following is indebted to those sources.

6. William Paley, *The Principles of Moral and Political Philosophy* (Indianapolis: Liberty Fund, 2002 [1755]); online: http://oll.libertyfund.org/Home3/Book.php?recordID=0158 (accessed 13/7/06), I.vi & II.v–vi.

7. Jeremy Bentham, I*ntroduction to the Principles of Morals and Legislation* (1789), I.i; online: http://www.la.utexas.edu/research/poltheory/bentham/ipml/index.html (accessed 13/7/06).

8. Jeremy Bentham, T*he Rationale of Reward* (1825); online: http://www.la.utexas.edu/research/poltheory/bentham/rr/index.html (accessed 13/7/06), III.i.

9. John Stuart Mill, 'Bentham', in *Dissertations and Discussion*, (1859); online: http://www.la.utexas.edu/research/poltheory/jsmill/diss–disc/bentham/bentham.html (accessed 13/7/06). Mill's other famous work, *Utilitarianism,* is also available at www.la.utexes.edu/research/poltheory/mil/util

10. The list is drawn from my general knowledge of Singer's work, but for two useful starting points see Peter Singer, *Rethinking Life and Death: The Collapse of Our Traditional Ethics* (Oxford: Oxford University Press, 1995) and Peter Singer, *Writings on an Ethical Life* (London: Fourth Estate, 2001). A Christian response to Singer's ethics can be found in Gordon Preece, ed. *Rethinking Peter Singer* (Downers Grove: IVP, 02).

11. Most of these points are drawn from Preece, pg 19. Point (iv) is my addition.

12. Quoted in Donald DeMarco, 'Peter Singer: Architect of the Culture of Death,' *Social Justice Review* 94 no. 9–10 (2003); online: www.catholiceducation.org/articles/medical_ethics/me0049.html (accessed 14/12/06).

13. Pope John Paul II, quoted in Demarco ibid.

14. Jonathan Glover, *Humanity: A Moral History of the Twentieth Century* (London: Pimlico, 1999), pg 107.

15. Robert E Goodin, 'Utility and the Good', in *A Companion to Ethics*, ed. Peter Singer (Oxford Blackwell 1991), pg 245.

16. For a brief summary, see Jenny Teichman, *Social Ethics: A Student's Guide* (Oxford: Blackwell, 1996), pgs 15–16. Also, William's reply to Smart, Smart and Williams, pgs 108–118, 124, 149–150.

17. The above discussion occurred on 'Cloning Clash' *Insight* SBS TV October 10, 2006 www.news.sbs.com.au/insight/search (14/12/06).

CHAPTER 5—HUMANISM

1. Francis Schaefffer, 'The God who is there,' in *The complete works of Francis Schaeffer, Vol 1,* (Crossway books, Wheaton, Illinois, 1982), pg 9.

2. The familiar motto 'Luna Park is just for fun' is found at www.lunaparksydney.com among many other websites about the history of Luna Park.

3. This quotation is from an article on the website of the *Humanist Society of Queensland*. www.hsq.aunz.com

4. See J. Herrick, *Humanism: An introduction* (Amherst, NY: Prometheus Books, 2005), pgs 5–6. Herrick writes: 'An astonishing explosion of art, philosophy and science took place in the fifth century BC in Greece.' This was the era that gave rise to philosophers such as Protagoras (481–422 BC), Socrates (469–399 BC), Plato (428–348 BC), Aristotle (384–322 B.), and Epicurus (341–271 BC). Herrick writes of Epicurus as 'perhaps the most important Greek philosopher from the humanist perspective ... He believed that the gods did not exist or at least were indifferent to humanity'.

5. S. E. Frost, *Basic teachings of the great philosophers*, (New York, NY: Anchor Books, 1989), pgs 62–63.

6. See Herrick, pgs 4–11.

7. The story of Prometheus is familiar. One account can be found at www.rohan.sdsu.edu/faculty/giftfire/prometheus

8. We are told that Prometheus was chained naked on a mountainside. Each day a gigantic eagle picked at his liver. In the evening the liver regrew and so the torture continued until he was freed generations later by Herakles. Prometheus endured his torture defiantly.

9. This quotation is taken from the *Prometheus Books* website, (accessed 10/8/06) www.prometheusbooks.com

10. P. Kurtz, (2004). 'Where is the good life? Making the humanist choice.' www.secularhumanism.org/library/fi/kurtz_18_3 (accessed 13/3/04)

11. S. Schafersman, (1998). 'The history and philosophy of humanism and its role in Unitarian Universalism.' www.freeinquiry.com/humanism-uu (accessed 22/6/06)

12. www.house-online.org/transcripts/transcripts episode1x05 (accessed 6/12/06)

13. Herrick, pg 5.

14. Kurtz, Where is the good life?

15. www.iheu.org/minimum_statement (accessed 21/7/06)

16. See the *Amsterdam Declaration of 2002*, reprinted in Herrick. The seven main points that are made are:

Humanism is ethical – morality is an intrinsic part of human nature based on understanding and a concern for others, needing no external sanction.

Humanism is rational – the solutions to the world's problems lie in human thought and action rather than divine intervention. Science and technology must be tempered by human values.

Humanism supports democracy and human rights—democracy and human development are rights.

Humanism insists that personal liberty must be combined with social responsibility—education must be free from indoctrination.

Humanism is a response to the widespread demand for an alternative to dogmatic religion.

Humanism values artistic creativity and recognises the transforming power of art —importance of literature, music and the visual and performing arts or personal development and fulfilment.

Humanism is a lifestyle aiming at the maximum possible fulfilment through the cultivation of ethical and creative living and offers an ethical and rational means of addressing the challenges of our times – it is a way of life for everyone.

17. See Herrick, pg 11. Herrick refers to Russell as a 'remarkable humanist'.

18. Ibid.

19. The term 'values' is used repeatedly in humanist literature. It is a subjective term, premised by the belief that there is nothing more substantial than the initiatives of human preference and decision-making in the area of morality. Humanism provides no foundations for belief in eternal laws or abiding norms for example, because there are no greater beings in the universe than evolved humans.

20. See P. Kurtz, *Humanist Manifesto 1 and 11* (Amherst, NY: Prometheus Books, 1973). In Humanist Manifesto 11, the following words concerning the origin and nature of ethics are written: 'We affirm that moral values derive their source from human experience. Ethics is *autonomous* and *situational*, needing no theological or ideological sanction, pg 17.

21. Schafersman freeinquiry.com/ humanism-uu

22. A.F. Holmes, 'Secular Humanism,' *New Dictionary of Christian Apologetics,* (Intervarsity Press, Downers Grove Illinois, 06), Pgs 654 – 655.

23. The text for the advertisement and the following market research extract are available from the Vodafone website www.vodafone.com (accessed 10/8/06).

24. Kurtz, Where is the good life?

25. Ibid.

26. Ibid.

27. There have been a number of important humanist statements in the twentieth and twenty-first centuries, including H*umanist Manifesto 1* (1933), *Humanist Manifesto 11* (1973), *A Secular Humanist Declaration* (1980), *A Declaration of Interdependence* (1988), *Humanist Manifesto 2000, and Humanist Manifesto 111* (2003). *The Amsterdam Declaration* (2002) has already been referred to and is another important humanist document.

28. Kurtz, *Humanist Manifestos 1 and 11*, pg 16.

29. Bertrand Russell quoted in Paul Johnson, *Intellectuals,* (Phoenix, Great Britain), pg 201.

30. B. Walsh and R. Middleton, *The transforming vision: Shaping a Christian worldview* (Downers Grove, IL: InterVarsity Press, 1985), pgs 31–32.

31. In Walsh and Middleton, ibid. pp 36-39

32. See Genesis 1:26–31 and Psalm 8 for example.

33. See Genesis 3 and following.

34. A.F. Holmes, 'Secular Humanism', *New Dictionary of Christian Apologetics,* (Intervarsity Press, Downers Grove Illinois, 06), pgs 654–655.

35. P. Kurtz, *Humanist Manifesto 2000: A call for a new planetary humanism* (Amherst, NY: Prometheus Books 2000), p 13.

36. *Humanist Manifesto 11* (1973) commenced with the following words:

   It is forty years since *Humanist Manifesto 1* (1933) appeared. Events since then make earlier statements seem far too optimistic. Nazism has shown the depths of brutality of which humanity is capable. Other totalitarian regimes have suppressed human rights without ending poverty. Science has sometimes brought evil as well as good. Recent decades have shown that inhuman wars can be made in the name of peace. The beginnings of police states, even in democratic societies, widespread government espionage, and other abuses of power by military, political, and industrial elites, and the continuance of unyielding racism, all present a different and difficult social outlook.

   There is no question about it. *Humanist Manifesto 1*, penned in the shadows of economic depression as even darker spectres of totalitarian oppression hovered over nations, and signed by leading humanist spokesmen such as American philosopher and educator John Dewey (1859–1952), was naively optimistic. However in 1973, with equal if not greater naivety, the authors of Humanist Manifesto 11 proceeded:

   As we approach the twenty-first century … an affirmative and hopeful vision is needed. Faith commensurate with advancing knowledge, is also necessary. In the choice between despair and hope, humanists respond in this Humanist Manifesto 11 with a positive declaration for times of uncertainty.

37. Kurtz, *Humanist Manifesto 2000,* pg 23.

38. Kurtz, Where is the good life?

39. In Frost, pg 78. The masculine terms 'mankind' and 'man' have been left unchanged so as to preserve the integrity of the quotation.

40. See Psalm 34:12 and following.

41. See John 10:10 and following.

42. As quoted by Pope John Paul 11 in his encyclical entitled *Evangelium Vitae.* Accessed on 17 August 2006 from www.usccb.org/prolife/programs/rlp/96rlpneu

43. www.objectivistcentre.org/cth-32-40-8-FAQ_is_Objectivism.aspx (accessed 5/12/06)

44. The survey was conducted by the Library of Congress and the Book-of-the-Month Club Members. The survey was based on 2032 responses and despite whatever limitations the survey contained, it does give a sense of the significance of the book in the lives of those who read it and for whom it resonated.

45. www.usatoday.com/money/companies/management/2002-09-23-ayn-rand_x.htm (accessed 5/12/06)

46. Quoted in Michael Shermer, *Why people believe weird things,* (W.H.

Freeman and Co. New York, 1997), pg 116.

47. Ibid.

CHAPTER 6—LIBERALISM

1. Gay, pg 52.

2. Kevin Rudd, 'What's Wrong With The Right: A Social Democratic Response To The Neo-liberals At Home And The Neo-conservatives Abroad', address to the Centre for Independent Studies, Sydney on 16 November 2006, Australian Federal Labor Party Website www.alp.org.au/media/1106/spefaistra160 (accessed 19/1/07).

3. Quoted in Rudd, ibid.

4. Robert Bellah et.al. quoted in Gay, pg 52.

5. John Locke, *An Essay Concerning Human Understanding* (1689, 1694).

6. MacIntyre, *Whose Justice? Which Rationality?* (Notre Dame: University of Notre Dame Press, 1988), pg 392.

7. Greg Melleuish 'The Paradox of power in the hands of liberals', *The Australian Financial Review*, news section, 15 July 2006, pg 62.

8. See for example Mary Ann Glendon's argument in *Rights Talk: The Impoverishment of Political Discourse* (New York: The Free Press, 1991).

9 Gay, pgs 54–55.

10. This scenario appeared in Philip Pettit, 'Consequentialism,' in Peter Singer (Ed) *A Companion to Ethics,* (Blackwell Publishers, Oxford UK, 1991), pg 231.

11. Ibid.

CHAPTER 7—FEMINISM

1. Ariel Levy, *Female Chauvinist Pigs* (Schwartz: Melbourne), pg 85.

2. Mary Wollstonecraft, 'A Vindication of the Rights of Women', chapter 11, www.bartleby.com/144/2

3. Ibid.

4. Mary Wollstonecraft, www.spartacus.schoolnet.co.uk/wollstonecraft.html (accessed 9/10/06).

5. Stanley Grenz and Denise Muir Kjesbo, *Women in the church: A biblical theology of women in the church* (Intervarsity Press, Downers Grove Illinois), pg 58.

6. Naomi Wolf, *Fire with fire: the new female power and how it will change the 21st eentury* (Chatto and Windus, London), pg 180.

7. Ibid.

8. Quoted in Michael and Auriel Schluter, 'Gender co-operation: some implications of God's design for society,' *Cambridge papers Jubilee Centre,* (Vol 12, No. 2 June 2003) www.jubilee-centre.org/online_documents/Gendercooperation (accessed 19/1/07).

9. For a comprehensive study of Australian first wave feminists see Susan Magarey, *Passions of the First Wave Feminists* (UNSW Press, 2002).

10. Doris Lessing quoted in Jane Cornwell, 'Beguiling', *The Weekend Australian*, 30–31 December 2006.

11. This fight documented in Levy, chapter 2: The future that never happened.

12. Wolf, pg xvi.

13. Quoted in 'Certain women,' Sydney Morning Herald *Good Weekend Magazine*, 28 October 2006.

14. Judith Whelan, editor's letter, *The Good Weekend*, 28 October 2006, pg13.

15. Wolf's book *Fire with Fire* devotes entire chapters to modern feminism's image problem.

16. Definitions taken from John G. Stackhouse, Jnr., *Finally Feminist: A Pragmatic Christian Understanding of Gender,* (Baker Academic, Grand Rapids Michigan, 2005) pg 17.

17. One of the major scholars in this area is Dr Marian C. Diamond, Professor of Anatomy/ Neuroanatomy at the University of California, Berkeley.

18. The prestigious Columbia University in New York now publishes a *Journal of Gender Specific Medicine*.

19. Stackhouse,*Finally Feminist*, pg 18.

20. Catherine Fox, 'A feminist's worst nightmare,' *Australian Financial Review*, 8 November 2005 www.newsstore.smh.com (accessed 13/6/06).

21. www.quotegarden.com/feminism (accessed 16/1/07)

22. Maxine Hancock, 'Christian Perspectives on Gender and Sexuality,' *CRUX* June 1999 vol XXXV No2, pg 8.

23. Rikki E Watts, 'Women in the Gospels and Acts,' *CRUX* June 1999 vol XXXV No2, pg 22.

24. John 4:4–42, the Samaritan woman encountering Jesus, Luke 10: 38–42, Mary at the feet of Jesus, the same student place in which Paul sat and learned at the feet of Gamaliel. Both of these narratives and others show how radical Jesus was in treating women with the same honour and opportunities with which he treated men.

25. See Wolf pgs 139–143 for a very interesting discussion of the relationship of the abortion issue and the feminist cause.

26. If one examines the Property Law Act debates in Victoria in 1958 the issues of married women having the right to own property apart from her husband still was being clarified within that particular Victorian state legislation. Less than 50 years ago this issue still was being clarified in Australian legislation.

27. Stackhouse, pg 17.

CHAPTER 8—RELATIVISM

1. Quoted in Douglas Groothius, 'Facing the Challenge of Postmodernism,' in F.J. Beckwith, W.L. Craig, and J.P. Moreland (Eds), *To everyone an answer, The case for a Christian Worldview – Essays in honour of Norman L. Geisler* (Intervarsity Press, Downers Grove, Illinois, 2004), pg 247.

2. Verses of Uplift (Udana) 68–69 (from the Suttapitaka. Khuddakanikalya). The translation is that of F. L. Woodward, The *Minor Anthologies of the Pali Canon* (Part II) (London: The Pali Text Society, 1987), pgs 82–83.

3. *The Macquarie Dictionary*, Third Edition (The Macquarie Library, 2001), pg 1798.

4. Plato, *Theaetetus* 152a6–8.

Protagoras' work is known only through the quotations in Plato.

5. Theaetetus 170a3–4.

6. Other philosophers who helped this relativist thought process along include Friedrich Nietzche (1844–1900) and Ludwig Wittgenstein (1889–1951). Today, two of the most famous relativist philosophers are Gilbert Harman of Princeton University (New Jersey, US) and his student David B. Wong now of Duke University (North Carolina, US).

7. Edward Rothstein, 'Attacks on the US Challenge Postmodern True Believers', New York Times, September 22, 2001. Quoted in Groothius, pg 251.

8. *Hansard,* House of Representatives, Monday 30 October 2006, 9:24pm, Sophie Mirabella MP (Indi, Victoria).

9. You can read the entire debate at: www.bringyou.to/apologetics/p20

10. For this view in the New Testament see Philippians 2:6–11.

11. For these views in the Quran see Sura 4.157–158 and 5.74–76.

12. John Hick, *The Rainbow of Faiths: Critical Dialogues on Religious Pluralism,* (London: SCM Press, 1995), pgs 24–25.

13. Steve Turner, *Up To Date* (London: Hodder and Stoughton, 1987), pgs 138–139.

14. From Gene Edward Veith, Jnr., *Postmodern Times – A Christian Guide to Contemporary Thought and Culture* (Crossway Books, Wheaton Illinois, 1994), pgs 44–46.

CHAPTER 9—NEW AGE

1. Quoted in Paul Heelas, *The New Age Movement* (Blackwell Publishers, Oxford, 1999), pg 15.

2. Quoted in Sheridan Voysey, *Unseen Footprints* (Scripture Union Australia, 2005), pg 32.

3. For more details see Ross Clifford and Philip Johnson, *Jesus and the gods of the New Age* (Colorado Springs, Victor, 2003), pgs 4–18.

4. Greg Tillett, *The Elder Brother: A biography of Charles Webster Leadbeate,* (London. Routledge & Kegan Paul, 1982), pg 4.

5. See Peter Proudfoot, *The Secret Plan of Canberra* (Kensington, University of New South Wales Press, 1994).

6. For a discussion on the Gnostic gospels Dan Brown relies on, and whether they are as reliable as the New Testament gospels, see Marc Rader, *Da Ciphering Da Vinci* (Bible Society NSW, 2006).

7. Kate Maver, 'Oprah Winfrey and her Self-Help Saviours: making the New Age Normal', *Christian Research Journal, 23, No.4* (2001): pgs 12–21.

8. See Shirley MacLaine, *Going Within* (New York, Bantan, 1989).

9. Clarissa Bye, 'The Future of Popcorn: An Interview', *The Sun-Herald*—Tempo, 21 January 2001, pg 5.

10. Wouter J. Hanegraaff, N*ew Age Religions and Western Culture: Esotericism in the Mirror of Secular Thought* (Albany, State University & New York Press, 1998), pg 517.

11. John Drane sees New Age

spirituality as the expression of the postmodern mindset. *What is the New Age Still Saying to the Church?* (London, Marshall Pickering, 1999), pgs 13–14.

12. See Philip Johnson and John Smulo, 'Reaching Wiccan and Mother Goddess Devotees' in *Encountering New Religious Movements,* eds. Irving Hexham, Stephen Rost, and John Morehead II (Grand Rapids, Kregel, 2004), pgs 209–225.

13. Paul Heelas, *The New Age Movement* (Blackwell Publishers, Oxford, 1999), pg 18.

14. Paul Heelas, *The New Age Movement: The Celebration of the Self and the Sacralization of Modernity* (Oxford, Blackwell, 1996), pg 159.

15. Neville Drury, *Exploring the Labyrinth: Making Sense of New Spirituality* (St.Leonards, Allen and Unwin, 1998), pg 98.

16. Fiona Horne, *Witch: A Personal Journey* (Sydney, Random House, 1998).

17. James Redfield, *The Celestine Prophecy* (Sydney, New York, London, Bantan Books, 1993), pg 98.

18. Rich Nathan, *Who is my enemy?* (Zondervan, Grand Rapids Michigan, 2002), pg 219.

19. Samantha Trenworth, *The Future of God* (Alexandria, Millennium, 1995), pgs x–xi.

20. *A Course in Miracles,* (London, Arkana, 1985), pg 172.

21. For a discussion and critique see Clifford and Johnson, *Jesus and the gods of the New Age,* chapter 11.

22. John P. Newport, *The New Age Movement and the Biblical Worldview* (Eerdmans Publishing, Grand Rapids Michigan, 1998), pg 46.

23. David Tacey, *The Edge of the Sacred* (Blacktown, Harper Collins, 1995), pg 192.

24. Doreen Virtue, *Angels 101* (Hay House Inc. USA, 2006), pg vii.

25. Ibid., pg xii.

26. James Sire, *The Universe Next Door – A basic worldview catalogue,* 4th Edition (Intervarsity Press, UK), pgs 174 – 175.

27. www.en.thinkexist.com/quotes/yoda (accessed 29/10/06)

28. John Dickson, *The Christ Files – How historians know what they know about Jesus* (Blue Bottle Books, Sydney, Australia, 2006).

29. J.R.R. Tolkien, 'On Fairy-Stories' in *Essays Presented to Charles Williams,* C.S. Lewis ed. (Grand Rapids, William B. Eerdmans, 1981), pgs 83–84.

30. www.lifepositive.com/mind/arts/new-age-fiction/fiction (accessed 31/10/06)

31. Eckart Tolle, *The Power of Now – A guide to spiritual enlightenment* (Hodder Australia, 2006), pg 12.

CHAPTER 10—CONSUMERISM

1. Abraham Joshua Heschel, *The Sabbath* (Farrar, Straus and Giroux, New York, 1951), pg 89.

2. Clive Hamilton, *Affluenza: When Too Much is Never Enough* (Crows Nest: Allen & Unwin, 2005). The term is originally taken from a PBS Documentary in the USA in 2003.

3. Skye Jethani, 'Leader's Insight: From Christ's Church to iChurch – How consumerism undermines our faith and community,' *Christianity Today Magazine* www.christianity today.com/leaders/newsletter/2006/clm60710 (accessed 17/11/06).

4. Rodney Clapp, 'Why the Devil Takes VISA,' *Christianity Today Magazine,* October 7 1996.

5. Elizabeth Hill, Lecturer in Political Economy at Sydney University assisted in condensing the economic theories of *commodification.*

6. Clapp.

7. Richard Eckersley, Ani Wierenga and Johanna Wyn, 'Success and wellbeing – a preview of the Australia 21 report on young people's wellbeing,' *Youth Studies Australia,* Vol. 25 Number 1, March 2006, pg 13.

8. Stuart and Elizabeth Ewen, quoted in David F. Wells *Above all earthly pow'rs – Christ in a Postmodern World* (Eerdmans Publishing, Grand Rapids Michigan, 2005), pg 18.

9. Walter Brueggemann, 'Enough is Enough,' *The Other Side* (Nov–Dec 2001), pg 13.

10. Sales of the planet saving 'Greenpower' remain at less than 1% of all electricity consumed in NSW.

11. Some writers have managed to meaningfully merge the two. See Paul Oslington, 'Natural Theology as an Integrative Framework for Economics and Theology,' St Mark's Day Public Lecture, St Mark's National Theological Centre, May 2005.

12. Naomi Klein, *No Logo* (Canada: Alfred A Knopf, 2001).

13. Quoted by Kate Betts, 'Luxury fever: how long will it last?', *Time Magazine* 'Style and development supplement', Fall 2004, pg 30.

14. Wells, pg 44.

15. Jeremy Carrette and Richard King, *Selling Spirituality: The Silent Takeover of Religion* (London: Routledge, 2005).

16. Rodney Clapp, 'Why the devil takes Visa' *Christianity Today Magazine,* October 7,1996

17. Jeffrey D. Sachs, *The End of Poverty: Economic Possibilities for our Time* (New York: Penguin, 2005).

18. Bono interviewed by Andrew Denton on *Enough Rope,* www.abc.net.au/tv/enoughrope/transcripts/s1777012

19. Vindana Shiva, 'How to end poverty: Making poverty history and the history of poverty' www.zmag.org/sustainers/content/2005-05/11shiva

20. Although closely related, globalisation is beyond the focus of this chapter.

21. Anon. Quoted in Hamilton, pg 19.

22. Jose Ortega y Gasset quoted in Gay, pg 44.

23. Charles Colson, 'The Back Pg: The Wages of Secularism,' *Christianity Today magazine,* www.ctlibrary.com/ct/2002/june10/27.64 (accessed 12/12/06).

24. Walter Brueggemann Miller P.D, 'The truth of abundance: relearning Dayenu *The covenanted self*

(Fortress Press, Minneapolis, 1999) pg 122.

25. The structure of the following summary loosely follows Craig L. Blomberg, *Neither Poverty nor Riches: A biblical theology of possessions* (Leicester: Apollos, 1999).

26. See John V Taylor, *Enough is enough* (London: SCM, 1975); Richard Foster, *Freedom of Simplicity*, 1981; Jacques Ellul, *Money and Power* (Downers Grove: IVP, 1984).

   And more recently Tom Beaudoin, *Consuming Faith: Integrating Who We Are with What We Buy*,(Lanham: Sheed & Ward, 2003); Brian Rosner, *Beyond Greed* (Kingsford: Matthais Media 2004); and the excellent book by Vincent J. Miller, *Consuming Religion: Christian Faith and Practice in a Consumer Culture* (London: Continuum, 2004).

27. Mike Hanley, 'The Happiness Guide', *Financial Review* 8/9/2006 pg 34.

28. Ibid.

29. Carolyn Jones, 'Out of the retail rat race – Consumer group doesn't buy notion that new is better', *San Francisco Chronicle* February 13, 2006 www.sfgate.com/cgi-bin/article.cgi?f=/c/a/2006/02/13/BAGH3H7DH71 (accessed 20/12/06)

about the authors

Simon Smart taught History and English for ten years before moving to Vancouver for theological study. He is a full-time writer for Anglican Youthworks and lives on Sydney's northern beaches with his wife and two children. He is a keen but inept surfer.

John Dickson is a busy public speaker and the author of 12 books. He teaches World Religions for the Macquarie Christian Studies Institute and is an Honorary Associate of the Department of Ancient History, Macquarie University.

Kirsten Birkett is an Australian who teaches at Oak Hill Theological College in London, UK, where she has discovered snow, fifty different varieties of rain but also bluebells. She's written a number of books and originally trained in the history and philosophy of science.

Greg Clarke is Director of the Centre for Apologetic Scholarship and Education at New College, University of New South Wales (www.case.edu.au). He writes and teaches about Christianity and culture, with a special interest in literature. Greg is the author of *Is It Worth Believing? The Spiritual Challenge of the Da Vinci Code*.

Andrew Cameron lectures in personal ethics, social ethics and philosophy at Sydney's Moore Theological College where he was a student in the early nineties. He is chairman of the Social Issues Executive of the Anglican Diocese of Sydney (http://your.sydneyanglicans.net/socialissues).

As well as working with various churches, Andrew studied Christian ethics in the United Kingdom. He likes playing computer games with his kids, wandering around his home suburb of Newtown with his wife Mary-Anne, the odd bike ride, and watching documentaries about nearly anything.

Rod Thompson was formerly Dean of the Department of Worldview Studies at Masters Institute in Auckland New Zealand. He currently lectures with the National Institute of Christian Education (NICE) in Sydney and speaks with teachers and parents about biblical foundations for education and schooling on behalf of Christian Parent Controlled Schools (CPCS). He lives with his wife Rosanne. Together they have four adult children.

David T. Koyzis is Professor of Political Science at Redeemer University College in Ancaster, Ontario, Canada, where he has taught since 1987. He is author of the award-winning *Political Visions and Illusions: A Survey and Christian Critique of Contemporary Ideologies*.

Mary Fisher became a Christian while a journalist at The Courier Mail in Brisbane. From 1977 she studied and worked in China and the USA.

In 1994 she joined the faculty of Asbury Theological Seminary in the USA working in the area of Biblical Theology. She left Asbury in 2005 and returned to Australia. Today she teaches at Macquarie Christian Studies Institute as well as being a pastoral worker at Sydney Chinese Alliance Church.

Michele Smart taught English and History in schools in the Sydney region before studying journalism. She went on to work for Law Press Australia and as a copywriter and then as an editor of various publications at APN Educational Media. She currently juggles freelance writing with being the mother of two small children.

Ross Clifford has his own talk back radio program that focuses on spiritual and ethical issues. He is the author of 8 books and he speaks often in churches and public forums. He is the Principal of Morling Theological and Bible College and lectures and writes on New Religious Movements. He is also the co-founder of Community of Hope that runs stalls in Mind-Body-Spirit festivals. In a past life he was a lawyer.

Geoff Broughton has spent the last decade living and ministering in the inner-city: Los Angeles, and Darlinghurst and Glebe in Sydney. He teaches courses on popular culture, and spirituality for everyday life for the Macquarie Christian Studies Institute and Youth Ministry for Moore Theological College. He is an ordained minister in the Anglican Church and a not-very-proficient sea-kayaker.